WILLIAMS-SONOMA

Weekends with Friends

GENERAL EDITOR

Chuck Williams

RECIPES

Betty Rosbottom

PHOTOGRAPHY

Joyce Oudkerk Pool

TIME
LIFE
BOOKS

TIME-LIFE BOOKS
Time-Life Books is a division of Time Life Inc.
Time-Life is a trademark of Time Warner Inc. U.S.A.

TIME-LIFE CUSTOM PUBLISHING
Vice President and Publisher: Neil Levin
Director of Financial Operations: J. Brian Birky
Director of Acquisitions: Jennifer L. Pearce

WILLIAMS-SONOMA
Founder and Vice-Chairman: Chuck Williams
Associate Book Buyer: Cecilia Michaelis

WELDON OWEN INC.
Chief Executive Officer: John Owen
President: Terry Newell
Vice President and Publisher: Wendely Harvey
Chief Operating Officer: Larry Partington
Vice President International Sales: Stuart Laurence
Series Editor: Val Cipollone
Managing Editor: Jan Newberry
Consulting Editor: Norman Kolpas
Copy Editor: Sharon Silva
Series Design: Kari Perin, Perin+Perin
Book Design: Diane Dempsey
Production Director: Stephanie Sherman
Production Manager: Christine DePedro
Production Editor: Sarah Lemas
Food Stylist: Andrea Lucich
Prop Stylist: Rebecca Stephany
Studio Assistant: Arjen Kammeraad
Food Styling Assistant: Elisabet der Nederlanden
Glossary Illustrations: Alice Harth

A NOTE ON WEIGHTS AND MEASURES
All recipes include customary U.S. and metric measurements. Metric conversions are based on a standard developed for these books and have been rounded off. Actual weights may vary.

The Williams-Sonoma Lifestyles Series
conceived and produced by Weldon Owen Inc.
814 Montgomery Street, San Francisco, CA 94133

In collaboration with Williams-Sonoma
3250 Van Ness Avenue, San Francisco, CA 94109

Separations by Colourscan Overseas Co. Pte. Ltd.
Printed in Singapore by Tien Wah Press (Pte.) Ltd.

A WELDON OWEN PRODUCTION
Copyright © 2000 Williams-Sonoma
    and Weldon Owen Inc.
All rights reserved, including the right of
reproduction in whole or in part in any form.

First printed in 2000
10 9 8 7 6 5 4 3 2 1

Library of Congress
Cataloging-in-Publication Data

Rosbottom, Betty
Weekends with friends / general editor, Chuck
  Williams; recipes by Betty Rosbottom; photography
  by Joyce Oudkerk Pool.
        p. cm. — (Williams-Sonoma lifestyles)
    Includes index.
    ISBN 0-7370-2031-8
    1. Cookery. I. Williams, Chuck.
  II. Title. III. Series.
  TX714.R658 2000
  641.5— dc21   99-43382
                                            CIP

MONOPOLY®, & © 2000 Hasbro, Inc.
Used with permission.

A NOTE ON NUTRITIONAL ANALYSIS
Each recipe is analyzed for significant nutrients per serving. Not included in the analysis are ingredients that are optional or added to taste, or are suggested as an alternative or substitution either in the recipe or in the recipe introduction or accompanying tip. In recipes that yield a range of servings, the analysis is for the middle of that range.

Contents

8 WELCOME TO THE WEEKEND

10 PLANNING WEEKEND MEALS   12 SETTING THE SCENE

14 BEVERAGES   16 PLANNING MENUS

18 Breakfast

38 Soups, Salads & Sandwiches

62 Dinner Main Courses

88 Desserts

108 GLOSSARY   112 INDEX

Welcome

Having friends visit for the weekend is one of the most enjoyable ways to entertain. It offers a leisurely chance to catch up on old times and to make new memories, often while gathered around the table for a meal.

But too many weekend hosts forget one essential ingredient for success: the need to make the experience as pleasurable for themselves as it is for their guests. They try to do too much, to make too grand an impression, and often end up spending more time at the stove than with their friends. That is why I find the recipes and ideas in this book such a refreshing change of pace. They recognize the fact that cooking for weekend visitors should and can be enjoyable and easy. Many of the dishes also make it possible for guests who love cooking to help out in the kitchen. The book's introductory pages provide a wealth of strategies for making the weekend flow smoothly, including tips for welcoming friends; suggestions for menu planning, shopping, and stocking the pantry; and ample inspiration for making every meal memorable.

The goal, in short, is a simple one: to make both you and your guests look forward with pleasure to the next weekend invitation.

Chuck Williams

Welcome to the Weekend

Ready for an afternoon arrival, Coconut Pound Cake (page 102) and a pitcher of Lemon-Mint Tea Coolers (page 14) await guests in the garden, where stacked wooden boxes form an impromptu serving table.

Setting a Welcoming Scene

The most important goal in weekend entertaining is to make your guests feel as comfortable in your home as possible. Whether they will be staying in a separate wing of the house or sleeping on a sofabed in the living room, there are simple steps you can take to make the stay pleasurable for both them and you.

Give some thought to where your guests will be sleeping. Before you make up beds with freshly laundered linens and spreads, give the mattresses an airing, if necessary, and plump the pillows. Add a few convenient and homey touches to the room: a notepad and pencil, a stack of interesting magazines or books, a radio, a vase of flowers. Such items help extend a heartfelt welcome. So, too, do a stack of fluffy towels and washcloths, a box of tissues, and a basket of little soaps, shampoo bottles, and other toiletries. Be sure, as well, to clear a spot for your guests to stow luggage and, if possible, provide a place where they can easily unpack.

And don't forget the bedside essentials of food and drink. Guests are always grateful to find a carafe or bottle of water and drinking glasses. Also consider setting out a bowl of fresh or dried fruits, a tin of cookies, or a box of chocolates, or try to recall what special snack foods your guests particularly crave and stock a personal pantry accordingly.

Greeting Guests with Food and Drink

When firming up weekend plans, establish as closely as possible what time your guests will arrive.

It makes good sense to avoid arrivals right around mealtimes, as greeting guests and helping them settle in can conflict with food preparation. Instead, aim for your visitors to show up mid-morning, in late afternoon, or after dinner.

With the time set, plan some simple foods and drinks to have on hand, ready to greet and refresh guests after their journey. Coffee and some simple baked goods are ideal in the morning. In the afternoon, the same baked goods and fresh fruit might accompany tea, brewed hot or iced depending upon the weather. For late-night arrivals, consider offering some sweet tidbits or a selection of cheeses along with a choice of coffee, dessert wine, brandy, or liqueurs.

Making Guests Feel at Home

Once your guests have settled in, put them at ease by discussing plans for the weekend, including a brief description of the meals you intend to serve. If they show any interest, invite them to participate in whatever last-minute planning, shopping, or food preparation remains to be done (see pages 10–11). Some guests may even offer to prepare their own specialties to add to the weekend table.

It's also a good idea to give guests a brief tour of the kitchen. Show them where they can find anything they might need, from fruit juices to breakfast cereals; coffee and tea supplies to the toaster, breads, and jams; cookies to ice creams, bowls, and toppings. Let them know that they are encouraged to help themselves.

To make things easier on yourself, give guests the option of helping keep things tidy by casually pointing out the location of dish detergents, kitchen towels, and the dishwasher. But don't expect them to be housekeepers. Be prepared to handle cleanup yourself.

The time of day and the season will suggest no end of possible welcoming gestures. On a bright midmorning, an impromptu light brunch (below, left) might include fresh berries and Double-Apricot Walnut Muffins (page 36) along with coffee and juice. A sweltering afternoon calls for a selection of soft drinks and beer kept well chilled in a galvanized tub filled with ice (above).

Planning Weekend Meals

Make advance planning for weekends with friends a pleasant task, enjoying a cup of tea and a cookie while you jot down your list of things to do (above). When shopping for the weekend (right), don't forget such essentials as beverages and flowers, as well as convenient ready-to-serve foods from bakeries or delicatessens.

Organizing with Guests in Mind
The first step in planning menus for a weekend with friends comes when you extend the invitation. Ask your guests if they have any special food requests. Are there favorite things they might like, or foods they don't particularly care for? Do they have any food allergies? Are they trying to reduce fat in their diets? (A nutritional analysis accompanies each recipe in the book.)

Information in hand, think through the weekend's activities and what types of meals might best complement them. A trip to the beach, for example, suggests a picnic. An event that everyone might want to watch on television calls for foods you can serve buffet style. A special occasion such as a birthday or an anniversary might demand a more formal multicourse menu.

Then, get out a pad of paper and a pencil and start mapping out the weekend, meal by meal. Do not be overly ambitious. Instead, aim for simple menus, featuring recipes that are fairly easy to cook, that can be prepared at least partially ahead, and that guests can pitch in and help to assemble if they like.

Don't overlook the role that convenience foods can play. One easy dinner at the end of a busy day, for example, could have as its centerpiece a whole chicken bought already roasted from a nearby market. Then all you need to do is prepare an appetizer and a few simple accompaniments.

Stocking the Weekend Pantry

Menus planned, you're ready to compile a shopping list of all the ingredients you'll need for the weekend. Don't forget to include beer, wine, sparkling water, and other beverages your guests might enjoy. Try to complete most of the shopping a day or two before your friends arrive, although you might want to save picking up some of the items for the weekend if you think any of your visitors would like seeing local specialty stores and farmers' markets.

While you're out, stock up on staples that don't necessarily appear on your menus, but that are sure to come in handy: coffee and teas, pasta and rice, such canned goods as tomatoes and tomato paste, cold cuts and condiments, and breakfast-table items such as eggs, milk, cereals, juices, fruit, breads, jams, and jellies.

Place a selection of snacks on hand, such as seasonal fruits and fresh-baked cookies, in the guest room or on a sideboard or coffee table for any guest who needs a quick pick-me-up.

Setting the Scene

Don't let a lack of time prevent you from sharing an elegant weekend dinner such as this menu featuring Lemon-Scented Roasted Chicken (page 63). Enlist the help of your guests to set the table with your best linens, glasses, silverware, and china.

Planning Morning Food

After a busy evening or gala dinner, everyone appreciates a simple morning menu served casually. Plan to make something that will hold well and can be served buffet style, such as muffins, scones, or coffee cake. Set the selections out on the kitchen, dining room, patio, or garden table along with plates, napkins, and cutlery. Include butter, jams, fresh fruits, juices, and thermoses of freshly brewed coffee and hot water with an array of teas.

Following a quieter evening, you may want to serve a more formal, sit-down breakfast or brunch of omelets, waffles, or other items that are completed and served once everyone has gathered. On a Sunday morning, be sure to leave a space on the table for the newspaper, which some of your guests are certain to want to read.

Making Lunchtime Convenient

Most weekends are likely to include some sort of daytime activity such as a walk in the park, swimming, tennis, or a visit to a museum. For that reason, lunch is most often a time for quick, convenient foods.

Even with convenience in mind, you can make the meal memorable by choosing the perfect setting. On a rainy afternoon, gather guests in front of a glowing fireplace to enjoy mugs of chowder. Seat everyone around a garden table on a sunny afternoon and enjoy salads and sandwiches outdoors.

And don't forget the pleasures of lunch packed to go. Transfer soup to a large thermos, wrap sandwiches airtight and keep them fresh in a cooler, pack brownies in a plastic container so they don't get smashed en route, and you have a memorable picnic ready to serve at the beach, after the tennis match, or on the museum lawn.

Serving Stylish Dinners

For most people, the evening meal will be the weekend's entertaining focal point. Dinner is usually eaten at a leisurely pace, allowing us to enjoy both the good food and the good company.

At this time of day, too, it makes sense to fashion the setting to both the occasion and the menu. For a special celebration, a formally set dining room is often in order, complete with your best china, glassware, cutlery, linens, flowers, place cards, and candlelight.

But dinner doesn't have to be formal. You can make an equally wonderful impression by serving a meal family style, bringing food to the dining room or kitchen table on large, rustic platters from which guests are encouraged to help themselves. Or lay out a buffet on the kitchen counter or on a sideboard and set up casual seating in the living or family room. Then let everyone scoop up their own servings of chili or lasagne before they take a seat wherever they choose.

The kitchen counter becomes an informal dinner buffet for guests to help themselves, with napkins, spoons, large bowls, beer, and wedges of corn bread all arrayed next to a steaming pot of Texas-Style Chili (page 78).

Beverages

Banana-Strawberry Smoothies

This refreshing drink is a perfect midafternoon treat. Serve it immediately, while it is still icy cold and frothy.

3 cups (12 oz/375 g) frozen unsweet-ened strawberries
2 ripe bananas, cut up
1½ cups (12 fl oz/375 ml) unsweet-ened pineapple juice
¼ cup (2 fl oz/60 ml) frozen orange juice concentrate
½ cup (4 fl oz/125 ml) good-quality vanilla ice cream
2 teaspoons vanilla extract (essence)
4 whole fresh strawberries
4 fresh mint sprigs

❈ In a blender or food processor, combine the frozen strawberries, bananas, pineapple juice, and orange juice concentrate. Process until smooth, 30–45 seconds. Add the ice cream and vanilla extract and process until thoroughly blended, 15–20 seconds.

❈ Pour into tumblers or large wineglasses. Float a strawberry on each drink, then garnish with a mint sprig. Serve immediately.

SERVES 4

Lemon-Mint Tea Coolers

Lemon and mint are natural partners. Serve this refreshing drink with or between meals. Store the tea, well covered, in the refrigerator for up to 3 days before serving.

2½ qt (2.5 l) water
4 lemon tea bags
1 mint tea bag
2–3 tablespoons sugar
ice cubes
10 lemon wedges, each ½ inch (12 mm) wide
10 fresh mint sprigs

❈ In a large nonaluminum saucepan over high heat, bring the water to a boil. As soon as it boils, remove from the heat and add the lemon and mint tea bags. Let steep for 25 minutes.

❈ Remove the bags and squeeze them over the saucepan to extract all the flavor. Taste and stir in the sugar as needed. Let cool completely, then cover and refrigerate for 1–2 hours to chill.

❈ To serve, fill tall glasses with ice cubes. Pour the tea over the ice to fill the glasses. Garnish each serving with a lemon wedge and a mint sprig.

SERVES 10

White and Dark Hot Chocolate

FOR THE WHITE CHOCOLATE
1½ oz (45 g) white chocolate, coarsely chopped
2 tablespoons plus ½ cup (4 fl oz/ 125 ml) heavy (double) cream

FOR THE DARK CHOCOLATE
7½ oz (235 g) semisweet (plain) chocolate, coarsely chopped
3 cups (24 fl oz/750 ml) milk

unsweetened cocoa powder

❊ To prepare the white chocolate, combine the white chocolate and the 2 tablespoons cream in a heatproof bowl placed over (not touching) simmering water in a saucepan. Whisk constantly until smooth, 1–2 minutes. Let cool.

❊ In a chilled bowl, whip the ½ cup (4 fl oz/125 ml) cream until soft peaks start to form. Add the cooled white chocolate mixture and continue to beat until stiff peaks form.

❊ To prepare the dark chocolate, in a heavy saucepan over low heat, combine the semisweet chocolate and milk. Whisk constantly until smooth, 3–4 minutes.

❊ To serve, fill mugs with the dark hot chocolate, dividing evenly. Top each with the white chocolate, again dividing evenly. Sprinkle with cocoa and serve immediately.

SERVES 4

Caramel Coffee with Cinnamon Cream

A touch of store-bought caramel sauce swirled together with hot brewed coffee is delicious served with a dollop of cinnamon-scented whipped cream.

1 cup (8 fl oz/250 ml) heavy (double) cream
1½ teaspoons light brown sugar
¼ teaspoon ground cinnamon, plus extra for garnish
¾ cup (6 fl oz/180 ml) caramel sauce
6 cups (48 fl oz/1.5 l) hot, strong brewed coffee
6 long cinnamon sticks (optional)

❊ In a chilled bowl, using an electric mixer set on medium speed or a whisk, whip the cream until soft peaks form. While continuing to beat, sprinkle in the brown sugar and the ¼ teaspoon ground cinnamon and beat for a few seconds longer to incorporate fully.

❊ Place 2 tablespoons of the caramel sauce in each of 6 coffee mugs or large coffee cups. Fill each cup three-fourths full with the hot coffee and stir well. Top each serving with a dollop of the flavored whipped cream and a sprinkling of ground cinnamon. Slip a cinnamon stick into each cup, if desired.

SERVES 6

Planning Menus

The ten menus provided here offer only a handful of the many combinations you can compose from the recipes that follow. When planning any menu, consider how much time you'd like to spend in the kitchen, whether it's important to include dishes that can be made ahead, or whether cooking as a group is on the activity list, in which case more time-sensitive or complicated menus are both possibilities.

Lazy Sunday Morning

Cinnamon French Toast
with Sautéed Bananas, Pecans,
and Maple Syrup
PAGE 33

Pan-fried Canadian Bacon

Fresh Orange Juice

Elegant Autumn Dinner

Pepper-and-Cumin-Coated
Lamb Chops
PAGE 77

Horseradish Mashed Potatoes
PAGE 73

Sautéed Zucchini

Fresh Figs and Pears

Late-Night Fare

Scrambled Eggs with
Smoked Salmon and
Herbed Cream Cheese
PAGE 26

Tossed Green Salad

Baguette

Champagne

Cold-Weather Buffet

Pasta Salad with Oranges,
Fennel, and Watercress
PAGE 49

Lemon-Scented Roasted Chicken
PAGE 63

Steamed Green Beans

Warm Pear and Dried
Cranberry Bread Pudding
PAGE 94

A Day at the Park

Turkey Burgers with
Jack Cheese and
Pepper-Corn Relish
PAGE 55

Corn on the Cob

Chocolate-Orange Brownies
PAGE 97

Garden Supper

Shrimp, Avocado, and Tomato
Salad with Lime Vinaigrette
PAGE 41

Skewers of Swordfish,
Red Peppers, and Oranges
PAGE 82

Couscous

Warm Plum Gratin
PAGE 91

Half-Time Menu

Corn Bread

Texas-Style Chili
PAGE 78

Coconut Pound Cake
with Vanilla Ice Cream and
Warm Chocolate Sauce
PAGE 102

Springtime Gathering

Fettuccine with Brie
and Asparagus
PAGE 64

Bread Sticks

Butter Lettuce Salad

Strawberry-Almond Tart
PAGE 101

Light Picnic Lunch

Garlic-Rubbed Baguette
with Chicken, Tomatoes,
and Tapenade
PAGE 46

Lemon-Mint Tea Coolers
PAGE 14

Extra-Thin, Extra-Crisp
Oatmeal Cookies
PAGE 104

Hearty Breakfast Fare

Country Omelets
with Potatoes, Leeks, and
Peppered Bacon
PAGE 20

Cranberry-and-Orange Scones
PAGE 29

Coffee or Tea

Ginger Waffles with Raspberry Sauce and Ginger Cream

PREP TIME: 45 MINUTES

COOKING TIME: 30 MINUTES

INGREDIENTS

FOR THE RASPBERRY SAUCE

¾ lb (375 g) fresh or frozen unsweetened raspberries, thawed but not drained if frozen

½ cup (4 oz/125 g) granulated sugar, or more to taste

FOR THE GINGER CREAM

1 cup (8 fl oz/250 ml) sour cream

¼ cup (2 oz/60 g) granulated sugar

1 teaspoon peeled and minced fresh ginger

1 teaspoon grated lemon zest

FOR THE WAFFLES

2¼ cups (9 oz/280 g) sifted all-purpose (plain) flour

1 tablespoon baking powder

3 eggs, separated

¼ cup (2 oz/60 g) firmly packed light brown sugar

1¾ cups (14 fl oz/430 ml) milk

6 tablespoons (3 oz/90 g) unsalted butter, melted

2 tablespoons peeled and minced fresh ginger

pinch of salt

½ pint (4 oz/125 g) fresh raspberries (optional)

fresh mint sprigs (optional)

Both the raspberry sauce and the ginger cream can be made a day ahead. Then all you need to do at breakfast time is prepare the batter, cook the waffles, and call your guests to the table.

SERVES 4

❀ To make the sauce, in a food processor or blender, process the berries and their juice until smooth, about 40 seconds. Strain through a sieve placed over a saucepan, pressing down with a spatula to extract as much liquid as possible. Discard the contents of the sieve. Add the ½ cup (4 oz/125 g) granulated sugar and place over medium heat. Stir until the sugar dissolves and the sauce is warm, 1–2 minutes. Taste and add more sugar, if needed.

❀ To make the ginger cream, in a small nonaluminum bowl, whisk together the sour cream, granulated sugar, ginger, and lemon zest. Cover and refrigerate until needed.

❀ Preheat an oven to 250°F (120°C). Preheat a waffle iron.

❀ To make the waffles, in a bowl, stir together the flour and baking powder. In another bowl, combine the egg yolks and brown sugar. Using an electric mixer set on medium speed, beat until smooth and thick, 2–3 minutes. Add the milk, melted butter, and ginger and mix well with a spoon. Gradually stir in the flour mixture until no lumps remain.

❀ In a clean bowl, with clean beaters, beat together the egg whites and salt until stiff peaks form. Gently fold into the batter.

❀ Ladle enough batter into the waffle iron for 1 waffle. Close the iron and cook until it opens easily or according to the manufacturer's directions. The waffle should be crisp and golden. As the waffles are cooked, transfer them to baking sheets, tent loosely with aluminum foil, and place in the warm oven.

❀ To serve, gently reheat the raspberry sauce. Serve the waffles drizzled with the warmed raspberry sauce and topped with a dollop of the ginger cream. Garnish, if desired, with raspberries and mint. Pass the remaining sauce and cream at the table.

NUTRITIONAL ANALYSIS PER SERVING: Calories 891 (Kilojoules 3,742); Protein 18 g; Carbohydrates 124 g; Total Fat 38 g; Saturated Fat 22 g; Cholesterol 246 mg; Sodium 540 mg; Dietary Fiber 6 g

Country Omelets with Potatoes, Leeks, and Peppered Bacon

PREP TIME: 20 MINUTES

COOKING TIME: 45 MINUTES

INGREDIENTS

FOR THE FILLING

6 slices thick-cut bacon, 6–8 oz
(185–250 g) total weight, cut
into ½-inch (12-mm) pieces

1½ teaspoons coarsely ground pepper

1 tablespoon unsalted butter

¾ lb (375 g) new potatoes, peeled
and cut into ½-inch (12-mm) dice

1 cup (4 oz/125 g) chopped leeks,
white part only

¼ teaspoon salt, plus salt to taste

½ cup (2 oz/60 g) shredded Gruyère
cheese

FOR THE OMELETS

8 eggs

½ teaspoon salt

4 teaspoons unsalted butter

3 tablespoons chopped fresh chives
or parsley, or a mixture

COOKING TIP: To ensure success,
use a nonstick pan and make sure
the butter is hot enough for the eggs
to set up quickly.

A sprinkle of grated Gruyère cheese complements the hearty
potato mixture that fills these robust omelets. Serve them as part
of a Sunday brunch or as a late-night meal for hungry travelers.

SERVES 4

❉ To make the filling, in a heavy frying pan over medium-high heat, fry
the bacon pieces until crisp and browned, 8–10 minutes. Using a slotted
spoon, transfer to paper towels to drain, then place in a small bowl. Add
the pepper and toss to coat the bacon evenly. Set aside.

❉ Pour off all but 1 tablespoon bacon fat from the pan and add the
butter. Place over medium heat until the butter melts and is hot. Add
the potatoes and cook, stirring, until slightly softened, about 3 minutes.
Add the leeks and the ¼ teaspoon salt and cook, stirring, until the leeks
begin to soften, about 2 minutes longer. Cover, reduce the heat to low,
and cook, stirring occasionally, until the potatoes are just tender, 8–10
minutes longer. Remove from the heat and season with salt to taste. Set
aside, uncovered. Set the cheese nearby.

❉ To make the omelets, in a bowl, whisk together the eggs and salt. The
omelets are quickly made, so it is best to serve each one as it is cooked.
Place an 8- or 9-inch (20- or 23-cm) nonstick frying pan over high heat
and add 1 teaspoon of the butter. As the butter melts, swirl the pan so the
butter covers the bottom and part of the sides. When the butter is quite
hot but not smoking, add one-fourth of the egg mixture and swirl to cover
the bottom of the pan evenly. Using a fork, gently and quickly stir the
eggs with a circular motion until set but still moist, about 2 minutes.

❉ Place one-fourth of the potato mixture on half of the omelet. Sprinkle
one-fourth each of the bacon and cheese over the potatoes. Using a spatula, flip the uncovered half of the omelet (near the handle) over onto the
filling. Lift the pan to slide the omelet onto a warmed individual plate.

❉ Sprinkle the omelet with one-fourth of the chives and/or parsley
and serve. Repeat to make 3 more omelets, using the remaining eggs,
butter, and herbs.

NUTRITIONAL ANALYSIS PER SERVING: Calories 452 (Kilojoules 1,898); Protein 23 g;
Carbohydrates 20 g; Total Fat 31 g; Saturated Fat 13 g; Cholesterol 473 mg; Sodium 857 mg;
Dietary Fiber 2 g

Dried Cherry and Almond Streusel Coffee Cake

PREP TIME: 45 MINUTES

COOKING TIME: 55 MINUTES,
   PLUS 15 MINUTES FOR
   COOLING

INGREDIENTS

FOR THE STREUSEL

1 cup (4 oz/125 g) dried sour cherries

1½ cups (12 fl oz/375 ml) hot water

⅔ cup (5 oz/155 g) firmly packed
   brown sugar

½ cup (2½ oz/75 g) all-purpose
   (plain) flour

¾ teaspoon ground cinnamon

½ cup (2½ oz/75 g) slivered blanched
   almonds, coarsely chopped

¼ cup (2 oz/60 g) chilled unsalted
   butter, cut into small pieces

FOR THE COFFEE CAKE

2⅔ cups (13½ oz/425 g) all-purpose
   (plain) flour

2 teaspoons baking powder

1 teaspoon baking soda (bicarbonate
   of soda)

rounded ¼ teaspoon salt

¾ cup (6 oz/185 g) unsalted butter,
   at room temperature

1 cup (8 oz/250 g) granulated sugar

3 eggs

1½ teaspoons almond extract
   (essence)

1 cup (8 fl oz/250 ml) sour cream

confectioners' (icing) sugar

With its swirls of cinnamon-and-almond streusel, this glorious, butter-rich coffee cake is ideal for serving large groups. Offer it at a late, leisurely breakfast or as a midafternoon snack.

SERVES 10–12

❀ Preheat an oven to 350°F (180°C). Butter and flour an 8½-inch (21.5-cm) bundt pan. Tap out excess flour.

❀ To make the streusel, in a bowl, combine the cherries and hot water. Let stand until softened, 5–10 minutes. Drain and set aside.

❀ Meanwhile, in a bowl, using a fork, toss together the brown sugar, flour, and cinnamon until well mixed. Using fingertips, mix in the almonds and butter until the mixture resembles coarse meal. Set aside.

❀ To make the coffee cake, in a bowl, briefly whisk together the flour, baking powder, baking soda, and salt. In another bowl, using an electric mixer set on medium-high speed, beat together the butter and granulated sugar until light, about 1 minute. Reduce the speed to low and add the eggs, one at a time, beating well after each addition. Add the almond extract and sour cream and beat until combined. Then gradually beat in the flour mixture.

❀ Pour one-third of the batter into the prepared pan. Top evenly with about one-third of the streusel mixture. Scatter half of the cherries over the streusel. Add another one-third of the batter, and top with half of the remaining streusel and all the remaining cherries. Top with the remaining batter and pat the remaining streusel evenly into the top.

❀ Bake until a cake tester inserted into the center comes out clean, 50–55 minutes. Remove from the oven and let cool in the pan on a rack for 15 minutes. Using a flexible spatula, loosen the cake from the pan sides. Invert a serving plate over the top of the pan, and invert the plate and pan together. Lift off the pan. Dust the cake with the confectioners' sugar. Serve warm or at room temperature.

NUTRITIONAL ANALYSIS PER SERVING: Calories 568 (Kilojoules 2,386); Protein 8 g; Carbohydrates 75 g; Total Fat 27 g; Saturated Fat 14 g; Cholesterol 114 mg; Sodium 304 mg; Dietary Fiber 2 g

Lemon Pancakes with Blueberry Sauce

PREP TIME: 30 MINUTES

COOKING TIME: 35 MINUTES

INGREDIENTS

FOR THE BLUEBERRY SAUCE

1 cup (8 fl oz/250 ml) water

5 tablespoons (3 fl oz/80 ml) lemon juice

2 tablespoons cornstarch (cornflour)

4 cups (1 lb/500 g) fresh or unsweetened frozen blueberries (thawed and well drained)

5 tablespoons (2½ oz/75 g) granulated sugar, or more to taste

⅛ teaspoon ground cinnamon

FOR THE PANCAKES

2 cups (10 oz/315 g) all-purpose (plain) flour

½ cup (4 oz/125 g) granulated sugar

2 teaspoons baking powder

1 teaspoon baking soda (bicarbonate of soda)

½ teaspoon salt

1½ cups (12 fl oz/375 ml) milk

1 cup (8 fl oz/250 ml) sour cream

2 eggs

6 tablespoons (3 oz/90 g) unsalted butter, melted and cooled

6 tablespoons (3 fl oz/90 ml) lemon juice

4½ teaspoons grated lemon zest

about 3 tablespoons vegetable oil or unsalted butter

confectioners' (icing) sugar

Drizzled with blueberry sauce, these golden flapjacks make a good, hearty breakfast before a day spent outdoors.

SERVES 6

❊ To make the blueberry sauce, in a saucepan over low heat, stir together the water, lemon juice, and cornstarch until the cornstarch dissolves, about 2 minutes. Add 2½ cups (10 oz/315 g) of the blueberries and raise the heat to medium. Cook, stirring, until the sauce thickens and coats a spoon, about 5 minutes. Let cool for 5–10 minutes, then transfer to a food processor or blender. Purée until smooth, then pass through a sieve placed over the saucepan, pressing down with a spatula to extract as much liquid as possible. Add the 5 tablespoons (2½ oz/75 g) granulated sugar and stir in the remaining 1½ cups (6 oz/185 g) blueberries. Place over medium heat and cook, stirring, until the berries soften slightly, 1–2 minutes. Stir in the cinnamon. Taste and add more sugar, if needed. Keep warm. You should have 2½ cups (20 fl oz/625 ml).

❊ Preheat an oven to 200°F (95°C).

❊ To make the pancakes, in a large bowl, whisk together the flour, granulated sugar, baking powder, baking soda, and salt. In another bowl, whisk together the milk, sour cream, eggs, melted butter, lemon juice, and 3 teaspoons of the zest. Pour the milk mixture over the flour mixture and stir just until combined. The batter will be lumpy.

❊ Place a griddle or large, heavy frying pan over medium heat. Brush lightly with some oil or butter. When hot, using a ¼-cup (2–fl oz/60-ml) measure, ladle the batter onto the griddle or pan; do not crowd the surface. Cook until small bubbles appear on the surface and the bottoms are lightly browned, 2–3 minutes. Flip the pancakes and cook until the second sides are lightly browned, 1–2 minutes longer. Transfer to a baking sheet in one layer, tent loosely with foil, and place in the warm oven. Repeat, using more oil or butter as needed. You should have 24 pancakes.

❊ To serve, gently reheat the sauce. Serve the pancakes on warmed individual plates. Ladle some of the warm sauce over them and sprinkle with the remaining 1½ teaspoons lemon zest, dividing evenly. Dust with the confectioners' sugar. Pass the remaining sauce at the table.

NUTRITIONAL ANALYSIS PER SERVING: Calories 656 (Kilojoules 2,755); Protein 11 g; Carbohydrates 87 g; Total Fat 31 g; Saturated Fat 15 g; Cholesterol 127 mg; Sodium 650 mg; Dietary Fiber 3 g

Scrambled Eggs with Smoked Salmon and Herbed Cream Cheese

PREP TIME: 10 MINUTES

COOKING TIME: 5 MINUTES

INGREDIENTS

8 eggs

3–4 oz (90–125 g) thinly sliced
smoked salmon, coarsely chopped

salt and ground pepper to taste

2 tablespoons unsalted butter

¼ lb (125 g) herbed cream cheese
such as Boursin, broken into small
chunks

2 tablespoons chopped fresh flat-leaf
(Italian) parsley or chives

COOKING TIP: The secret to creamy,
moist scrambled eggs is not to over-
cook them. Scramble them until they
are just set, rather than lumpy and dry.

The classic combination of smoked salmon and cream cheese,
often served at brunch to welcome weekend visitors, is even
better when combined with scrambled eggs. Split and toast
some onion bagels and serve alongside. Open a bottle of your
best champagne and make the meal a celebration.

SERVES 4

❀ In a bowl, whisk the eggs lightly just to blend. Add the salmon and
stir to mix. Season lightly with salt and pepper.

❀ In a large, heavy frying pan over medium heat, melt the butter.
When hot, pour in the egg mixture and cook, stirring constantly, until
the eggs start to set, about 2 minutes. Sprinkle the cheese evenly over
the eggs and continue to cook and stir until the eggs are scrambled to
a soft consistency, about 1 minute longer. Taste and season with more
salt, if needed.

❀ Transfer to a warmed platter. Sprinkle with additional pepper and
then with the parsley or chives. Serve immediately.

NUTRITIONAL ANALYSIS PER SERVING: Calories 335 (Kilojoules 1,407); Protein 19 g;
Carbohydrates 2 g; Total Fat 26 g; Saturated Fat 13 g; Cholesterol 472 mg; Sodium 813 mg;
Dietary Fiber 0 g

Cranberry-and-Orange Scones

PREP TIME: 30 MINUTES

COOKING TIME: 15 MINUTES

INGREDIENTS

3 tablespoons dried cranberries

½ cup (4 fl oz/125 ml) orange juice, heated

1 tablespoon thawed frozen orange juice concentrate

1½ cups (7½ oz/235 g) all-purpose (plain) flour

1½ tablespoons sugar

½ teaspoon baking powder

¼ teaspoon salt

7 tablespoons (3½ oz/105 g) chilled unsalted butter, cut into small pieces

1 egg, lightly beaten

1½ tablespoons grated orange zest

MAKE-AHEAD TIP: Although these scones are best served piping hot from the oven, they can be baked ahead. Store them in an airtight container for up to 2 days, then cover with aluminum foil and reheat in a preheated 300°F (150°C) oven for about 10 minutes.

One of these scrumptious biscuit-sized scones is never enough. Served hot and spread with butter, they are a wonderful complement to scrambled eggs or omelets. Or you can set them out in the afternoon with a pot of tea or coffee.

MAKES 10–12 SCONES

✾ Preheat an oven to 400°F (200°C).

✾ In a small bowl, combine the cranberries and heated orange juice. Let stand until softened, about 10 minutes, then drain over a small bowl, reserving the juice. Chop the cranberries roughly and set aside.

✾ In another small bowl, combine the orange juice concentrate with 2 tablespoons of the reserved juice. Set aside. Save any remaining juice.

✾ In a bowl, whisk together the flour, sugar, baking powder, and salt. Cut in the butter with a pastry blender or 2 knives until the mixture resembles rolled oats. Add the egg and mix well with a fork. Add the reserved orange juice concentrate mixture, the cranberries, and the orange zest. Mix only until a soft dough forms. If the dough is dry, add the reserved juice as needed.

✾ On a floured work surface, roll out the dough into a round ½ inch (12 mm) thick. Using a round cookie cutter 2 inches (5 cm) in diameter, cut out as many scones as possible. Gather the dough scraps together, roll out again, and cut out as many more as possible. You should have 10–12 scones. Place them on an ungreased baking sheet.

✾ Bake until lightly golden, about 15 minutes. Watch carefully so that the bottoms do not burn. Transfer to a rack and let cool for 2–3 minutes. Serve hot.

NUTRITIONAL ANALYSIS PER SCONE: Calories 168 (Kilojoules 706); Protein 3 g; Carbohydrates 21 g; Total Fat 8 g; Saturated Fat 5 g; Cholesterol 39 mg; Sodium 81 mg; Dietary Fiber 1 g

Pepper Jack Cornmeal Pancakes with Tomato Salsa

PREP TIME: 25 MINUTES

COOKING TIME: 20 MINUTES

INGREDIENTS

FOR THE SALSA

6 ripe plum (Roma) tomatoes,
  halved, seeded, and cut into
  ½-inch (12-mm) dice

⅔ cup (2 oz/60 g) chopped green
  (spring) onions (about 12), including 2 inches (5 cm) of green tops

2 or 3 jalapeño chiles, seeded and
  finely diced

2 tablespoons chopped fresh
  cilantro (fresh coriander)

2 tablespoons lime juice

½ teaspoon salt, or more to taste

FOR THE PANCAKES

2 cups (10 oz/315 g) yellow cornmeal

1 cup (5 oz/155 g) all-purpose
  (plain) flour

1 tablespoon baking powder

1 teaspoon salt

⅔ cup (2½ oz/75 g) finely shredded
  pepper jack cheese

2 cups (16 fl oz/500 ml) milk, plus
  up to ½ cup (4 fl oz/125 ml)
  more, if needed

4 eggs, lightly beaten

¼ cup (2 oz/60 g) unsalted butter,
  melted and cooled

2–3 tablespoons vegetable oil

6 tablespoons (3 fl oz/90 ml) sour
  cream

Cornmeal adds a crunchy texture to the griddle cakes, while the pepper jack cheese provides a spicy accent. These brunch pancakes can also be served as evening appetizers accompanied with cold beer or margaritas.

SERVES 6

❁ To make the salsa, in a bowl, stir together the tomatoes, green onions, jalapeños, cilantro, lime juice, and ½ teaspoon salt. Taste and add more salt, if needed. You should have about 3 cups (24 fl oz/750 ml). Set aside.

❁ Preheat an oven to 200°F (95°C). Have ready 2 baking sheets and aluminum foil.

❁ To make the pancakes, in a large bowl, whisk together the cornmeal, flour, baking powder, and salt. Add the cheese and toss to mix. In another bowl, whisk together the 2 cups (16 fl oz/500 ml) milk, eggs, and butter. Pour the milk mixture over the flour mixture and stir just until combined. If the batter seems too thick, add a little more milk to thin. It should be the consistency of yogurt.

❁ Place a griddle or large, heavy frying pan over medium heat. Brush lightly with vegetable oil. When hot, using a ¼-cup (2–fl oz/60-ml) mea-sure, ladle the batter onto the griddle or frying pan. Cook the pancakes until small bubbles appear on the surface and the bottoms are a light golden brown, about 1½ minutes. Using a spatula, flip the pancakes and cook until the second sides are a light golden brown and the pancakes are just cooked through, 1–2 minutes longer. As the pancakes are cooked, transfer to a baking sheet in one layer, tent loosely with foil, and place in the warm oven. Repeat, using more oil as needed, until all the batter is used. You should have about 18 pancakes.

❁ To serve, place 3 pancakes on each warmed individual plate. Spoon ⅓ cup (3 fl oz/80 ml) salsa onto each serving, and top each with about 1 tablespoon of the sour cream. Pass the remaining salsa at the table.

NUTRITIONAL ANALYSIS PER SERVING: Calories 582 (Kilojoules 2,444); Protein 18 g; Carbohydrates 65 g; Total Fat 28 g; Saturated Fat 13 g; Cholesterol 195 mg; Sodium 1,013 mg; Dietary Fiber 4 g

Cinnamon French Toast with Sautéed Bananas, Pecans, and Maple Syrup

PREP TIME: 25 MINUTES

COOKING TIME: 20 MINUTES

INGREDIENTS

⅓ cup (1½ oz/45 g) pecan halves

4 eggs

1 cup (8 fl oz/250 ml) milk

1 teaspoon ground cinnamon

8 slices good-quality day-old white bread, each about ½ inch (12 mm) thick

1 tablespoon unsalted butter, or as needed

1 tablespoon vegetable oil, or as needed

FOR THE TOPPING

1½ tablespoons unsalted butter

3 large, ripe bananas, peeled and cut into slices ¼ inch (6 mm) thick

sprinkle of ground cinnamon

1 cup (11 fl oz/345 ml) pure maple syrup, heated

COOKING TIP: The success of this dish depends in part on using real maple syrup, which has a rich, complex flavor that marries well with the bananas and nuts.

Fuel up for a day of cross-country skiing or other winter sports with this cinnamon-scented French toast. Panfried Canadian bacon or sausage links would make fine accompaniments. If you like, substitute walnut halves or slivered almonds for the pecans.

SERVES 4

✿ Preheat an oven to 350°F (180°C). Spread the pecans on a baking sheet and toast in the oven until golden and fragrant, 5–8 minutes. Remove from the oven, let cool, and chop coarsely. Set aside. Reduce the oven temperature to 250°F (120°C).

✿ In a bowl, whisk together the eggs, milk, and cinnamon until blended. Pour into a large, shallow glass or ceramic dish and add enough bread slices to fit comfortably. Soak the slices, turning once, for a few seconds total. Carefully transfer the slices to a plate and repeat until all the slices are soaked.

✿ Have ready a baking sheet. In a large, heavy frying pan or griddle over medium-low heat, warm ½ tablespoon each of the butter and the vegetable oil. When hot, add enough bread slices to fit comfortably in a single layer and cook until golden brown on the bottoms, about 2 minutes. Turn over the toasts and cook until golden brown on the second sides, about 2 minutes longer. Transfer to the baking sheet and place in the warm oven. Repeat until all the soaked bread is cooked, adding more butter and oil in equal amounts as needed.

✿ To make the topping, in a large, heavy frying pan over medium-high heat, melt the butter. When hot, add the sliced bananas and sauté, stirring constantly, until warm, about 1 minute. Remove from the heat.

✿ To serve, place 2 toasts on each warmed individual plate. Top with the sautéed bananas, dividing evenly. Sprinkle each serving with some cinnamon and toasted nuts, then drizzle with some of the maple syrup. Pass the remaining syrup at the table.

NUTRITIONAL ANALYSIS PER SERVING: Calories 723 (Kilojoules 3,037); Protein 15 g; Carbohydrates 109 g; Total Fat 27 g; Saturated Fat 9 g; Cholesterol 241 mg; Sodium 407 mg; Dietary Fiber 4 g

Gratin of Eggs with Mushrooms, Rosemary, and Parmesan

PREP TIME: 25 MINUTES

COOKING TIME: 50 MINUTES

INGREDIENTS

2 tablespoons unsalted butter

½ lb (250 g) fresh white mushrooms, brushed clean and coarsely chopped

½ lb (250 g) fresh shiitake mushrooms, brushed clean, stems discarded, and caps coarsely chopped

1 tablespoon minced garlic

½ teaspoon dried thyme

¾ teaspoon chopped fresh rosemary or ¼ teaspoon dried rosemary, plus fresh sprigs for garnish (optional)

rounded ½ teaspoon salt

¼ teaspoon ground pepper

1 cup (8 fl oz/250 ml) reduced-sodium chicken broth

6 eggs

1½ cups (12 fl oz/375 ml) half-and-half (half cream)

¾ cup (3 oz/90 g) grated Parmesan cheese, preferably Parmigiano-Reggiano

COOKING TIP: For a richer taste and smoother texture, use heavy (double) cream in place of the half-and-half.

An easy-to-assemble centerpiece for brunch, this gratin goes well with warmed crusty French bread and a selection of jams. The dish holds beautifully, covered, for up to 30 minutes after it comes out of the oven. Serve with slices of country ham and steamed asparagus spears drizzled with lemon juice.

SERVES 4–6

❀ Position an oven rack in the lower third of an oven and preheat to 350°F (180°C). Lightly butter a shallow 1½-qt (48–fl oz/1.5-l) baking dish.

❀ In a large, heavy frying pan over medium-high heat, melt the butter. When hot, add the white and shiitake mushrooms and sauté, stirring constantly, until the liquid released from the mushrooms has evaporated and the mushrooms are lightly browned, 5–6 minutes. Add the garlic, thyme, rosemary, salt, and pepper. Stir and cook for 1 minute longer.

❀ Add the broth and bring to a simmer. Cook, stirring constantly, until all the liquid has evaporated, about 4 minutes. Taste and adjust the seasonings. Remove from the heat and let cool for 5–10 minutes.

❀ In a large bowl, whisk together the eggs and half-and-half just until blended. Gradually add the mushroom mixture, mixing well to combine. Stir in the cheese. Transfer to the prepared baking dish.

❀ Bake until just golden on top and a wooden pick inserted into the center comes out clean, 30–35 minutes. If the top has not browned sufficiently, turn on the broiler (griller) and broil (grill) for a few minutes until golden. Let stand for 10 minutes before serving. Garnish the top with rosemary sprigs, if you like, and cut into squares to serve.

NUTRITIONAL ANALYSIS PER SERVING: Calories 324 (Kilojoules 1,361); Protein 17 g; Carbohydrates 8 g; Total Fat 25 g; Saturated Fat 14 g; Cholesterol 311 mg; Sodium 607 mg; Dietary Fiber 1 g

Double-Apricot Walnut Muffins

PREP TIME: 30 MINUTES

COOKING TIME: 30 MINUTES

INGREDIENTS

FOR THE TOPPING

1 tablespoon sugar

¼ teaspoon ground cinnamon

FOR THE MUFFINS

⅔ cup (2½ oz/75 g) walnuts

⅔ cup (4 oz/125 g) dried apricots

1 cup (8 fl oz/250 ml) hot water

2 cups (10 oz/315 g) all-purpose (plain) flour

½ cup (4 oz/125 g) plus 2 tablespoons sugar

1 tablespoon baking powder

1½ teaspoons ground cinnamon

1 teaspoon salt

¾ cup (6 fl oz/180 ml) milk

2 eggs, lightly beaten

6 tablespoons (3 oz/90 g) unsalted butter, melted and cooled

1 teaspoon vanilla extract (essence)

¼ cup (2½ oz/75 g) apricot preserves

COOKING TIP: To make removing the muffins from the pan easier, butter the flat top surface of the pan as well as the insides of the molds.

An unexpected burst of flavor—a dollop of apricot preserves—is baked into the center of each muffin. Serve with bowls of granola and yogurt as a light breakfast for late sleepers or with hot tea or coffee for a midafternoon break.

MAKES 12 MUFFINS

❀ Preheat an oven to 350°F (180°C). Butter a 12-cup standard muffin pan.

❀ To make the topping, in a small bowl, stir together the sugar and cinnamon. Set aside.

❀ To make the muffins, spread the walnuts on a baking sheet and toast in the oven until they take on color and are fragrant, 5–8 minutes. Remove from the oven, let cool, and chop. Raise the oven temperature to 400°F (200°C).

❀ Meanwhile, in a bowl, combine the apricots and hot water. Let stand until softened, about 10 minutes. Drain, pat dry thoroughly with paper towels, and chop roughly.

❀ In a large bowl, briefly whisk together the flour, sugar, baking powder, cinnamon, salt, and walnuts. Add the apricots and toss to coat with the flour mixture.

❀ In another bowl, whisk together the milk, eggs, butter, and vanilla until well blended. Pour the milk mixture over the flour mixture and stir just to combine. Fill each prepared muffin cup halfway full with batter. Place about 1 teaspoon preserves on top of each half-filled cup, and poke it down slightly. Add the remaining batter to fill each cup. Sprinkle the tops with the cinnamon-sugar topping, dividing evenly.

❀ Bake until puffed and golden, 15–18 minutes. Remove from the oven and turn out onto a rack to cool slightly. Serve hot.

NUTRITIONAL ANALYSIS PER MUFFIN: Calories 289 (Kilojoules 1,214); Protein 5 g; Carbohydrates 42 g; Total Fat 12 g; Saturated Fat 5 g; Cholesterol 56 mg; Sodium 340 mg; Dietary Fiber 2 g

Tomato Soup with Minted Goat Cheese

PREP TIME: 30 MINUTES

COOKING TIME: 45 MINUTES

INGREDIENTS

3 tablespoons olive oil

2 cups (10 oz/315 g) chopped
  yellow onion

1 cup (5 oz/155 g) peeled and diced
  carrot

1 tablespoon chopped garlic

2 cans (28 oz/875 g each) plum
  (Roma) tomatoes, drained well
  and coarsely chopped

3½–4 cups (28–32 fl oz/875 ml–1 l)
  chicken broth

1 teaspoon salt

⅛ teaspoon cayenne pepper

FOR THE GOAT CHEESE GARNISH

5 oz (155 g) creamy fresh goat
  cheese

2–3 tablespoons milk

4 teaspoons chopped fresh mint

MAKE-AHEAD TIP: This soup
improves in flavor when made a day
ahead and reheated. The garnish can
be prepared 1 day ahead, covered,
and refrigerated. Bring to room
temperature before using.

Topped with creamy white goat cheese, this deep red tomato soup looks far more complicated to assemble than its simple preparation proves. A hint of cayenne delivers a peppery accent, while chopped mint adds a refreshing note.

SERVES 4

❋ In a large, deep-sided nonaluminum saucepan over medium heat, warm the olive oil. When hot, add the onion and carrot and sauté, stirring, until beginning to soften, about 3 minutes. Add the garlic and sauté, stirring, for 1 minute longer. Add the tomatoes, 3½ cups (28 fl oz/875 ml) broth, salt, and cayenne pepper. Bring to a simmer, reduce the heat to low, and simmer, uncovered, until all the vegetables are tender, 30–35 minutes.

❋ Remove from the heat and let cool for 10 minutes. Working in batches, purée in a food processor or blender until smooth. Return the soup to the saucepan over medium heat and heat to serving temperature, about 5 minutes. If the soup is too thick, thin with the remaining ½ cup (4 fl oz/125 ml) broth. Taste and adjust the seasonings.

❋ To make the garnish, place the cheese in a small nonaluminum bowl. Whisk in the milk, 1 tablespoon at a time, until the mixture is smooth and the consistency of a medium-thick sauce. You may not need all of the milk.

❋ To serve, ladle the soup into warmed bowls. Drizzle each serving with about 3 tablespoons of the goat cheese, forming a zigzag pattern. Garnish each serving with 1 teaspoon mint.

NUTRITIONAL ANALYSIS PER SERVING: Calories 345 (Kilojoules 1,449); Protein 14 g; Carbohydrates 29 g; Total Fat 21 g; Saturated Fat 7 g; Cholesterol 18 mg; Sodium 2,318 mg; Dietary Fiber 6 g

Shrimp, Avocado, and Tomato Salad with Lime Vinaigrette

PREP TIME: 40 MINUTES

COOKING TIME: 5 MINUTES

INGREDIENTS

FOR THE VINAIGRETTE

2 tablespoons lime juice

2 teaspoons ground cumin

1½ teaspoons grated lime zest

1 teaspoon minced garlic

½ teaspoon Dijon mustard

½ teaspoon salt

¼ teaspoon ground pepper

5 tablespoons (2½ fl oz/75 ml)
  olive oil

FOR THE SALAD

24 large shrimp (prawns) in the shell,
  1–1¼ lb (500–625 g) total weight

2 ripe avocados

6 small yellow or red tomatoes or
  a combination of the two, about
  ¾ lb (375 g) total weight

3 tablespoons chopped fresh
  cilantro (fresh coriander)

6 cups (9 oz/280 g) packed mixed
  salad greens

ground pepper to taste

MAKE-AHEAD TIP: The dressing
can be made up to 2 hours ahead.
Cover and let stand at cool room
temperature.

Cumin adds an unexpected but pleasing flavor to the lime vinaigrette. This salad is equally good served as a first course or as a light lunch on a busy day when you're planning a big evening meal for your guests.

SERVES 6

❈ To make the vinaigrette, whisk together the lime juice, cumin, lime zest, garlic, mustard, salt, and pepper. Whisk in the olive oil. Set aside.

❈ To make the salad, bring a saucepan three-fourths full of water to a boil. Add the shrimp and cook until they curl and turn pink, about 3 minutes. Drain and pat dry. Peel and devein and place in a large non-aluminum bowl. Add half of the vinaigrette to the shrimp, toss well, and let stand for 10 minutes.

❈ Meanwhile, halve, pit, and peel the avocados and cut lengthwise into slices ½ inch (12 mm) thick. Core and halve the tomatoes and cut into wedges ½ inch (12 mm) wide. Add the avocados, tomatoes, and cilantro to the shrimp and toss gently.

❈ Place the salad greens in a separate bowl. Whisk the remaining vinaigrette and pour over the greens. Toss well. Divide the greens among individual plates. Top with the shrimp mixture. Season each serving with several grinds of pepper and serve at once.

NUTRITIONAL ANALYSIS PER SERVING: Calories 310 (Kilojoules 1,302); Protein 17 g; Carbohydrates 11 g; Total Fat 23 g; Saturated Fat 3 g; Cholesterol 106 mg; Sodium 329 mg; Dietary Fiber 3 g

Grilled Fontina and Prosciutto Sandwiches

PREP TIME: 15 MINUTES

COOKING TIME: 10 MINUTES

INGREDIENTS

8 large slices coarse country bread, each about ½ inch (12 mm) thick

5–6 oz (155–185 g) Italian fontina cheese, sliced

4 thin slices prosciutto, about 2 oz (60 g) total weight

2 teaspoons chopped fresh rosemary or 1½ teaspoons dried rosemary, plus 4 fresh sprigs (optional)

about 3 tablespoons olive oil

12–16 mixed black and green olives

COOKING TIP: When the weather is nice, try cooking these sandwiches on an outdoor grill. Before grilling, press down gently but firmly on each sandwich to help seal it, and brush the outer surface of both sides with the olive oil.

Ordinary grilled cheese sandwiches become a special lunch for weekend visitors when you use an out-of-the-ordinary filling. Italian fontina, called Fontina Val d'Aosta, makes the most satisfying sandwich. Rich and creamy, it has a slightly nutty taste and melts beautifully. Fontinas made elsewhere tend to be less flavorful. In late summer, set out fresh figs with the sandwiches.

SERVES 4

❀ Place 4 slices of the bread on a work surface. Divide the cheese evenly among them, top each with a slice of prosciutto, and then sprinkle with the chopped or dried rosemary, again dividing evenly. Cover with the remaining bread slices.

❀ In a large, heavy frying pan, pour in enough of the olive oil to form a film on the bottom, and place over medium-high heat. When hot, add as many sandwiches as will fit comfortably in the pan and cook, pressing down often with a metal spatula, until golden brown on the bottoms, 2–3 minutes. Turn over the sandwiches, adding more oil to the pan if necessary to prevent scorching. Cook, again pressing down on the sandwiches, until golden brown on the second sides, about 2 minutes longer. Transfer to a plate and repeat with the remaining sandwiches, adding more oil to the pan as needed.

❀ Cut the sandwiches on the diagonal. Garnish with the olives and with the rosemary sprigs, if using. Serve hot.

NUTRITIONAL ANALYSIS PER SERVING: Calories 453 (Kilojoules 1,903); Protein 19 g; Carbohydrates 31 g; Total Fat 28 g; Saturated Fat 10 g; Cholesterol 57 mg; Sodium 1,146 mg; Dietary Fiber 2 g

Mushroom, Carrot, and Leek Soup with Shaved Parmesan

PREP TIME: 45 MINUTES

COOKING TIME: 30 MINUTES

INGREDIENTS

2 tablespoons unsalted butter

2 tablespoons vegetable oil

4 carrots, peeled and cut into
   julienne strips 3 inches (7.5 cm)
   long by ¼ inch (6 mm) wide by
   ¼ inch (6 mm) thick

2 leeks, white part only, halved
   lengthwise and sliced crosswise
   ¼ inch (6 mm) thick

1 lb (500 g) fresh shiitake mushrooms,
   brushed clean, stems discarded, and
   caps cut into julienne strips ¼ inch
   (6 mm) wide

¼ lb (125 g) white fresh mushrooms,
   brushed clean and thinly sliced

2 teaspoons finely chopped garlic

3 cups (24 fl oz/750 ml) beef broth

3 cups (24 fl oz/750 ml) chicken
   broth

½ teaspoon salt

¼ teaspoon ground pepper

wedge of Parmesan cheese,
   preferably Parmigiano-Reggiano,
   4–6 ounces (125–185 g)

4 fresh flat-leaf (Italian) parsley sprigs

MAKE-AHEAD TIP: The soup can be
made 1 day in advance, covered, and
refrigerated. Reheat over medium heat.

This light, flavorful soup is perfect to precede a main course.
The broth, a combination of rich chicken and beef broths, carries
a colorful array of finely cut vegetables.

SERVES 4

❀ In a large, deep-sided saucepan over medium-high heat, melt the butter with the vegetable oil. When hot, add the carrots and cook, stirring,
until slightly softened, 2–3 minutes. Add the leeks and cook, stirring,
until slightly softened, 3–4 minutes longer. Add the shiitake and white
mushrooms and the garlic and cook, stirring, until softened and beginning to wilt, about 5 minutes.

❀ Add the beef and chicken broths, salt, and pepper, and simmer,
uncovered, until all the vegetables are tender, about 15 minutes. Taste
and adjust the seasonings.

❀ To serve, ladle into warmed individual bowls. Using a vegetable peeler
or cheese slicer, shave thin slices from the wedge of Parmesan.
Generously garnish each serving with the cheese and a parsley sprig.

NUTRITIONAL ANALYSIS PER SERVING: Calories 385 (Kilojoules 1,617); Protein 19 g;
Carbohydrates 23 g; Total Fat 25 g; Saturated Fat 13 g; Cholesterol 49 mg; Sodium 1,919 mg;
Dietary Fiber 5 g

Garlic-Rubbed Baguette with Chicken, Tomatoes, and Tapenade

PREP TIME: 25 MINUTES

INGREDIENTS

1 baguette, 24 inches (60 cm) long and 2½ inches (6 cm) in diameter

3 tablespoons extra-virgin olive oil

1 large clove garlic, halved

¼ lb (125 g) creamy fresh goat cheese

about ¼ cup (2 oz/60 g) store-bought tapenade *(see note)*

1 roasted chicken, 2½–3 lb (1.25–1.5 kg), at room temperature, skin removed and meat sliced *(see note)*

2 or 3 plum (Roma) tomatoes, sliced

leaves from 1 small bunch fresh basil

ground pepper to taste

SERVING TIP: If you plan to serve these sandwiches at a picnic and won't be eating them right away, pack all the components separately—including the grilled garlic-rubbed bread halves—and assemble the sandwiches just before guests are ready to eat.

Roasted chicken, either store-bought or home-cooked like the Lemon-Scented Roasted Chicken on page 63, is put to good use in these sandwiches, which also call for store-bought tapenade. The latter, a Provençal condiment, is a pastelike mixture of olives, capers, anchovies, olive oil, lemon juice, and seasonings. It is sold in jars in specialty-food shops and some well-stocked food stores. Pack the sandwiches for a picnic at the beach or for lunch at an afternoon concert in the park.

MAKES 4 SANDWICHES

❀ Place the baguette on a work surface and cut on the diagonal into 4 equal pieces. Cut each piece in half horizontally. Brush the cut surfaces with the olive oil.

❀ Place a stove-top grill pan over medium heat. When hot, place the bread, cut sides down, on the pan and grill until lightly browned, about 1 minute. Remove from the pan and rub the cut surfaces with the cut sides of the garlic clove.

❀ Spread the 4 bottom pieces of bread generously with the goat cheese, dividing it evenly. Smear a thin layer of the tapenade over the cheese. Place the sliced chicken over the tapenade, and top with the tomato slices and several fresh basil leaves. Grind some fresh pepper over all. Close the sandwiches and serve at once.

NUTRITIONAL ANALYSIS PER SANDWICH: Calories 774 (Kilojoules 3,251); Protein 62 g; Carbohydrates 46 g; Total Fat 36 g; Saturated Fat 10 g; Cholesterol 164 mg; Sodium 1,161 mg; Dietary Fiber 3 g

Pasta Salad with Oranges, Fennel, and Watercress

PREP TIME: 45 MINUTES

COOKING TIME: 15 MINUTES

INGREDIENTS

FOR THE DRESSING

¼ cup (2 fl oz/60 ml) plus 1½ teaspoons orange juice

¼ cup (2 fl oz/60 ml) plus 1½ teaspoons white wine vinegar

1 tablespoon grated orange zest

¾ teaspoon salt

ground pepper to taste

3 tablespoons olive oil

FOR THE SALAD

1 lb (500 g) penne or other tube-
shaped dried pasta

2 fennel bulbs

24 brine-cured black olives such as
Kalamata, pitted and slivered

½ lb (250 g) feta cheese, crumbled

2 navel oranges

1 bunch watercress, tough stems
removed (about 3 cups/3 oz/90 g
tender leaves and stems)

PREP TIP: A cherry pitter is the ideal
tool for pitting the olives.

Ideal for serving in the cooler months when oranges and fennel are at their best, this hearty salad can be partnered with soup for lunch or supper or set out as a side dish on a buffet. The recipe can easily be increased for larger gatherings.

SERVES 6

❀ To make the dressing, in a small bowl, whisk together the orange juice, vinegar, orange zest, salt, and a few grinds of pepper. Whisk in the olive oil. (The dressing can be made up to 2 hours ahead. Cover and let stand at cool room temperature.)

❀ To make the salad, bring a large saucepan three-fourths full of salted water to a boil. Add the pasta, stir well, and cook until al dente (tender, yet still firm to the bite), about 12 minutes or according to package directions. Drain well, rinse with cold water until cool, and drain well again. Transfer to a large bowl.

❀ Working with 1 fennel bulb at a time, cut off the stems and feathery tops and any bruised outer stalks. Halve lengthwise, cut away the tough core portion, and cut into narrow julienne strips. Add to the pasta along with the olives and cheese. Toss well to combine. Whisk the dressing and pour half of it over the pasta. Stir to coat well. Let stand for 5 minutes or for up to 1 hour at cool room temperature.

❀ Working with 1 orange at a time and using a small, sharp knife, cut a slice off the top and bottom to expose the fruit. Place upright on the cutting board and thickly slice off the peel in strips, cutting around the contour of the orange to expose the flesh. Holding the orange over a bowl, cut along either side of each section to free it from the membrane, letting the section drop into the bowl.

❀ Just before serving, add the orange sections, watercress, and the remaining dressing to the pasta mixture. Mix gently. Taste and adjust the seasonings, then serve.

NUTRITIONAL ANALYSIS PER SERVING: Calories 548 (Kilojoules 2,302); Protein 17 g; Carbohydrates 71 g; Total Fat 21 g; Saturated Fat 7 g; Cholesterol 34 mg; Sodium 1,187 mg; Dietary Fiber 4 g

Grilled Tuna, White Bean, and Arugula Salad

PREP TIME: 45 MINUTES, PLUS
2 HOURS FOR MARINATING

COOKING TIME: 5 MINUTES,
PLUS PREPARING FIRE

INGREDIENTS

1 fennel bulb

3 cans (15 oz/470 g each) cannellini
beans, rinsed, drained, and
patted dry

6 plum (Roma) tomatoes, halved,
seeded, and cut into ½-inch
(12-mm) dice

1 cup (4 oz/125 g) chopped sweet
red (Spanish) onion

15 brine-cured black olives such as
Kalamata, pitted and slivered

6 tablespoons (3 fl oz/90 ml) lemon
juice

2 teaspoons finely chopped garlic

1½ teaspoons dried thyme

1 teaspoon salt, plus salt to taste

¼ teaspoon ground pepper, plus
pepper to taste

¾ cup (6 fl oz/180 ml) olive oil

1½ lb (750 g) tuna fillet, about ¾ inch
(2 cm) thick

2 teaspoons soy sauce

½ lb (250 g) arugula (rocket), tough
stems removed

2 teaspoons grated lemon zest

This main-course salad, dressed with a lemon-garlic vinaigrette, is the perfect luncheon centerpiece for your just-arrived summertime guests. The fish can also be cooked in a broiler (griller) using the same timing.

SERVES 6

❋ Cut off the stems and feathery tops and any bruised outer stalks from the fennel bulb. Quarter lengthwise, cut away the tough core portion, and dice. Place in a large nonaluminum bowl. Add the beans, tomatoes, onion, and olives and mix well.

❋ In a small bowl, whisk together 4 tablespoons (2 fl oz/60 ml) of the lemon juice, the garlic, thyme, the 1 teaspoon salt, and the ¼ teaspoon pepper. Whisk in the olive oil to form a dressing. Remove and reserve ¼ cup (2 fl oz/60 ml). Add the remaining dressing to the bean mixture, toss well, and marinate for at least 2 hours or for up to 4 hours.

❋ About 45 minutes before serving, place the tuna in a shallow glass dish. Add the soy sauce to the reserved dressing, and pour over the tuna. Cover and let stand at cool room temperature.

❋ Prepare a medium-hot fire in a charcoal grill.

❋ When the coals are ready, remove the tuna from the marinade and place on the oiled grill rack 4–5 inches (10–13 cm) above the fire. Grill, turning once, until seared on the outside but still pink at the center, 1½–2 minutes on each side, or until done to your liking. Remove from the grill rack and sprinkle lightly with salt and pepper. Cut into slices about ¼ inch (6 mm) thick.

❋ Meanwhile, reserve one-third of the arugula and set aside. Roughly chop the remaining arugula and add to the bean mixture. Mix well. Taste and adjust the seasonings.

❋ To serve, arrange one-sixth of the reserved arugula on one side of each individual plate. Mound one-sixth of the salad in the center of each plate and arrange the tuna on top, dividing evenly. Drizzle the remaining lemon juice over the tuna, then sprinkle with the lemon zest. Serve at once.

NUTRITIONAL ANALYSIS PER SERVING: Calories 597 (Kilojoules 2,507); Protein 37 g; Carbohydrates 34 g; Total Fat 35 g; Saturated Fat 5 g; Cholesterol 39 mg; Sodium 1,052 mg; Dietary Fiber 11 g

Corn and Lobster Chowder

PREP TIME: 35 MINUTES

COOKING TIME: 25 MINUTES

INGREDIENTS

2 tablespoons vegetable oil

1½ cups (6 oz/185 g) chopped leeks, white part only

3 cups (18 oz/560 g) corn kernels (from about 6 ears)

1 teaspoon dried thyme

½ teaspoon salt

⅛ teaspoon cayenne pepper

⅛ teaspoon ground nutmeg

3½–4 cups (28–32 fl oz/875 ml–1 l) chicken broth

2 Yukon gold potatoes, about 1 lb (500 g) total weight, peeled and cut into ½-inch (12-mm) dice

½ cup (4 fl oz/125 ml) half-and-half (half cream)

1 tablespoon unsalted butter

¾ lb (375 g) cooked lobster meat, cut into large chunks, plus extra for garnish

1½ tablespoons chopped fresh flat-leaf (Italian) parsley

COOKING TIP: Purchase cooked lobster meat from a reputable fishmonger. Or buy live lobsters, cook them, and remove the meat yourself. Plan on 1 pound (500 g) of lobster to yield ¼ pound (125 g) cooked meat.

Old-fashioned corn chowder is elevated to new culinary heights when chunks of rosy lobster meat are added just before serving. Peeled and deveined raw shrimp (prawns) can replace the lobster in this recipe. Use 3 large shrimp per serving (18 total). Sauté in 1–2 tablespoons vegetable oil until pink and curled, about 3 minutes. This soup is ideal for a late-summer supper after a day at the beach. Serve the chowder with a mixed green salad and warmed bread.

SERVES 6

❊ In a large, heavy, deep-sided saucepan over medium heat, warm the vegetable oil. When hot, add the leeks and 2½ cups (15 oz/470 g) of the corn kernels and sauté, stirring, until beginning to soften, about 3 minutes. Add the thyme, salt, cayenne, nutmeg, and 3 cups (24 fl oz/750 ml) of the broth. Bring to a simmer, then reduce the heat to low and cook gently.

❊ Meanwhile, in a food processor or blender, combine the remaining ½ cup (3 oz/90 g) corn and ½ cup (4 fl oz/125 ml) broth. Purée until smooth. Stir the puréed mixture into the simmering soup along with the potatoes. Cook, uncovered, until the potatoes and corn are tender but still slightly firm, about 15 minutes.

❊ Stir in the half-and-half, then taste and adjust the seasonings. If the soup is too thick, thin with the remaining ½ cup (4 fl oz/125 ml) broth.

❊ In a heavy frying pan over medium heat, melt the butter. When hot, add the ¾ lb (375 g) lobster meat and sauté to heat through, 1–2 minutes.

❊ Ladle the soup into warmed shallow bowls. Garnish the center of each serving with some lobster and sprinkle with parsley.

NUTRITIONAL ANALYSIS PER SERVING: Calories 304 (Kilojoules 1,277); Protein 18 g; Carbohydrates 35 g; Total Fat 12 g; Saturated Fat 4 g; Cholesterol 53 mg; Sodium 1,066 mg; Dietary Fiber 4 g

Turkey Burgers with Jack Cheese and Pepper-Corn Relish

PREP TIME: 30 MINUTES,
PLUS 1 HOUR STANDING
TIME FOR RELISH

COOKING TIME: 10 MINUTES

INGREDIENTS

FOR THE RELISH

1 teaspoon olive oil

1 cup (6 oz/185 g) corn kernels
(from about 2 ears)

1 red bell pepper (capsicum), seeded
and chopped (⅔ cup/3½ oz/105 g)

6 tablespoons (2 oz/60 g) finely
chopped sweet red (Spanish)
onion

1¼ teaspoons minced garlic

⅛ teaspoon salt

⅛ teaspoon ground black pepper

1½ tablespoons lime juice

1½ tablespoons chopped fresh
cilantro (fresh coriander)

FOR THE BURGERS

1 lb (500 g) ground (minced) turkey
or chicken

2 teaspoons ground cumin

1½ teaspoons grated lime zest

1½ teaspoons lime juice

¾ teaspoon salt

⅛ teaspoon cayenne pepper

8 thin slices pepper jack cheese

4 good-quality hamburger buns or
French rolls, split and lightly toasted

Burgers made with ground turkey and seasoned with cumin, lime, and cayenne are lower in fat than traditional beef burgers. The piquant pepper-corn relish adds both flavor and color. Cook the burgers on an outdoor grill, if you like.

SERVES 4

❀ To make the relish, in a large, heavy frying pan over medium heat, warm the olive oil. When hot, add the corn and bell pepper and cook, stirring constantly, for 5 minutes. Add the onion and garlic and cook, stirring, until the onion is softened, about 3 minutes. Stir in the salt and black pepper. Remove the mixture from the heat, transfer to a nonaluminum bowl, and stir in the lime juice and cilantro. Taste and adjust the seasonings. Cover and let stand at room temperature for 1 hour. (The relish can be prepared 4–5 hours ahead, covered, and refrigerated. Bring to room temperature 30 minutes before using.)

❀ Meanwhile, make the burgers: In a bowl, combine the turkey or chicken, cumin, lime zest and juice, salt, and cayenne pepper. Mix well to blend. Divide into 4 portions and shape each portion into a patty ½ inch (12 mm) thick. Cover and refrigerate for at least 30 minutes or for up to 5 hours.

❀ When ready to serve, spray a large, heavy frying pan with nonstick cooking spray and place over medium heat. When hot, add the patties and cook, turning once, until cooked throughout, about 4 minutes on each side. Place 2 slices of the cheese on each patty and cook until the cheese melts, about 1 minute longer.

❀ Place the hamburger buns on individual plates, cut sides up. Transfer the burgers to the bottom halves of the buns, top with the relish, and top with the other halves of the buns. Pass the extra relish at the table.

NUTRITIONAL ANALYSIS PER SERVING: Calories 491 (Kilojoules 2,062); Protein 33 g; Carbohydrates 35 g; Total Fat 25 g; Saturated Fat 9 g; Cholesterol 87 mg; Sodium 1,020 mg; Dietary Fiber 3 g

Pita Pockets with Pork, Red Onion, and Chutney Mayonnaise

PREP TIME: 30 MINUTES, PLUS
6½ HOURS IF MARINATING
AND GRILLING PORK

INGREDIENTS

FOR THE CHUTNEY MAYONNAISE

1 cup (8 fl oz/250 ml) mayonnaise

¼ cup (2½ oz/75 g) mango chutney

2 teaspoons finely chopped green
(spring) onion, including tender
green tops

2 teaspoons peeled and grated fresh
ginger

½ teaspoon curry powder

ground pepper to taste

FOR THE SANDWICHES

6 pita breads, each 6 inches (15 cm)
in diameter

¾–1 lb (375–500 g) cooked pork
tenderloin, thinly sliced (*see note*)

1 red (Spanish) onion, thinly sliced

1 cup (1½ oz/45 g) packed spinach
leaves, preferably baby spinach

HEALTHY TIP: Good-quality reduced-
fat mayonnaise (but not nonfat, which
lacks flavor) works fine in this recipe.

Prepare these pita pockets when an informal lunch or supper is on your weekend schedule. For the pork, buy an extra tenderloin and increase the marinade accordingly when you prepare Orange-Ginger Pork Tenderloins (page 69). Alternatively, use leftovers from another favorite recipe.

SERVES 6

✻ To make the chutney mayonnaise, in a nonaluminum bowl, combine the mayonnaise, chutney, green onion, ginger, curry powder, and pepper. Stir to mix well. Cover and refrigerate if not using immediately.

✻ To assemble the sandwiches, cut each pita bread in half to create 2 half-moon pockets. Spread the inside of each pita half with a generous 1½ tablespoons of the chutney mayonnaise. Divide the pork evenly among the pita halves, then add a few onion slices and some spinach to each.

✻ Arrange the pita halves in a napkin-lined basket or on a platter and serve at once.

NUTRITIONAL ANALYSIS PER SERVING: Calories 618 (Kilojoules 2,596); Protein 27 g; Carbohydrates 47 g; Total Fat 36 g; Saturated Fat 6 g; Cholesterol 84 mg; Sodium 704 mg; Dietary Fiber 2 g

Butternut Squash Soup with Caramelized Onions, White Beans, and Escarole

PREP TIME: 30 MINUTES

COOKING TIME: 35 MINUTES

INGREDIENTS

3 tablespoons unsalted butter

3 or 4 yellow onions, thinly sliced (about 5 cups/18 oz/560 g)

1 teaspoon sugar

1 butternut squash, halved, seeded, peeled and cut into ½-inch (12-mm) dice

¼ lb (125 g) good-quality smoked ham such as Black Forest, cut into ½-inch (12-mm) dice

2½ teaspoons dried thyme

1½ teaspoons dried rosemary

¾ teaspoon dried sage

5 cups (40 fl oz/1.25 l) reduced-sodium chicken broth

¾ teaspoon salt

½ teaspoon ground pepper

1 can (15 oz/470 g) Great Northern white beans, rinsed and well drained

2 cups (6 oz/185 g) coarsely chopped escarole (Batavian endive)

1 cup (5 oz/155 g) frozen tiny green peas, thawed

1 cup (4 oz/125 g) shredded provolone cheese

Escarole, although only an accent in this soup, adds an important flavor. A member of the endive family, it has broad, slightly curved green leaves and a milder flavor than its cousin, Belgian endive (chicory/witloof). Available year-round, it is at its prime from early summer to early autumn. Serve the robust soup as a main course, either for lunch or supper. Complete the meal with a salad and a plate of Extra-Thin, Extra-Crisp Oatmeal Cookies (page 104).

SERVES 6

❄ In a deep-sided, heavy saucepan over medium heat, melt the butter. When hot, add the onions and sprinkle with the sugar. Cook slowly, stirring, until the onions start to brown, about 10 minutes. Add the squash, ham, thyme, rosemary, and sage and cook, stirring, until the squash softens slightly, about 4 minutes longer. Add the broth, salt, and pepper and bring to a simmer. Reduce the heat to low and simmer, uncovered, until the squash is barely tender, 8–12 minutes.

❄ Add the beans and escarole and cook until the escarole is completely wilted, about 5 minutes. (The soup can be made 1 day ahead up to this point. Let cool, cover, and refrigerate, then reheat over medium heat, stirring occasionally, before continuing.) Add the peas and cook just until heated through, about 2 minutes. Taste and adjust the seasonings.

❄ Ladle into warmed bowls and garnish each serving with a generous sprinkling of cheese. Serve immediately.

NUTRITIONAL ANALYSIS PER SERVING: Calories 320 (Kilojoules 1,344); Protein 17 g; Carbohydrates 36 g; Total Fat 13 g; Saturated Fat 7 g; Cholesterol 37 mg; Sodium 1,353 mg; Dietary Fiber 8 g

Sliced Flank Steak, Haricot Vert, and Potato Salad

PREP TIME: 25 MINUTES,
PLUS GRILLING STEAK

COOKING TIME: 25 MINUTES

INGREDIENTS

FOR THE DRESSING

¼ cup (2 fl oz/60 ml) red wine vinegar

¼ cup (1½ oz/45 g) minced shallot

2 teaspoons Dijon mustard

1 teaspoon salt

1 teaspoon ground pepper

½ cup (4 fl oz/125 ml) olive oil

FOR THE SALAD

⅔ lb (315 g) haricots verts, trimmed and left whole, or other young, tender green beans, trimmed and cut on the diagonal into 2-inch (5-cm) lengths

2 lb (1 kg) red potatoes, unpeeled

2½ teaspoons chopped fresh thyme leaves

2 teaspoons chopped fresh rosemary leaves

salt and ground pepper to taste

1 lb (500 g) flank steak, grilled (see note), at room temperature

6 tablespoons (2 oz/60 g) crumbled blue cheese such as Roquefort

HEALTHY TIP: Crumbled feta makes a delicious, lower-fat substitute for the blue cheese.

Place an extra steak over the coals when you prepare Grilled Flank Steak with Horseradish Mashed Potatoes (page 73) and serve this salad the next day. Corn on the cob and sliced tomatoes sprinkled with basil round out the menu for a casual outdoor lunch.

SERVES 6

✹ To make the dressing, in a small bowl, whisk together the vinegar, shallot, mustard, salt, and pepper. Whisk in the olive oil. (The dressing can be made up to 2 hours ahead. Cover and let stand at cool room temperature.)

✹ Bring a large pot of lightly salted water to a boil. Add the beans and boil until just tender, 3–4 minutes for haricots verts or 5 minutes or longer for larger beans. Using a slotted spoon, scoop out the beans and place under cold running water to halt the cooking and set the color. Pat dry with paper towels and set aside.

✹ Return the water to a boil and add the potatoes. Boil until easily pierced with a sharp knife, 15–20 minutes. Drain. (The beans and potatoes can be prepared up to 3 hours ahead. Cover and keep at cool room temperature.)

✹ When cool enough to handle, cut the cooked potatoes into 1-inch (2.5-cm) cubes. Place them in a large nonaluminum bowl along with the beans. Whisk the dressing and pour two-thirds of it over the potatoes and beans. Sprinkle with the thyme, rosemary, salt, and pepper and mix well. Taste and adjust the seasonings.

✹ Slice the steak against the grain into slices ¼ inch (6 mm) thick, then cut each slice in half lengthwise.

✹ To serve, divide the potato and bean mixture evenly among individual plates. Divide the steak strips and mound in the center of each portion. Drizzle the meat with the remaining dressing, and sprinkle each serving with 1 tablespoon blue cheese.

NUTRITIONAL ANALYSIS PER SERVING: Calories 465 (Kilojoules 1,953); Protein 21 g; Carbohydrates 32 g; Total Fat 28 g; Saturated Fat 7 g; Cholesterol 46 mg; Sodium 660 mg; Dietary Fiber 4 g

Lemon-Scented Roasted Chicken

PREP TIME: 15 MINUTES

COOKING TIME: 1½ HOURS

INGREDIENTS

1 chicken, 3½–4 lb (1.75–2 kg)

salt and ground pepper to taste

1 small bunch fresh rosemary

3 lemons

1 tablespoon olive oil

1⅓ cups (11 fl oz/320 ml) reduced-
   sodium chicken broth, or as needed

¼ cup (2 fl oz/60 ml) heavy (double)
   cream, or as needed

COOKING TIP: When you thicken the
pan drippings and broth, the liquid
reduces, but the amount of salt
remains the same. That is why it is
important to use reduced-sodium
broth, or the sauce will be too salty.

A whole lemon baked in the cavity infuses this golden bird with
a light citrus taste. Accompany the chicken with roasted potatoes
and English peas braised with green (spring) onions.

SERVES 4

❀ Position an oven rack in the lower third of an oven and preheat to
375°F (190°C).

❀ Rinse the chicken and remove any excess fat. Pat the cavity dry and
season it with salt and pepper. Place 2 or 3 rosemary sprigs and 1 whole
unpeeled lemon in the cavity and skewer it closed. Tuck the wing tips
underneath the breasts, then cross the drumsticks and, using kitchen
string, tie the legs tightly together. Place the chicken, breast up, on a
rack in a heavy roasting pan. Rub the olive oil over the entire surface
of the chicken. Pour ⅓ cup (3 fl oz/80 ml) of the broth into the pan.

❀ Roast for 45 minutes. Squeeze the juice of 1 lemon over the chicken,
and then pour ⅓ cup (3 fl oz/80 ml) of the broth over the chicken. Continue
to roast until the skin is a rich golden brown and an instant-read thermometer inserted into the thickest part of the thigh away from the bone
registers 180°F (82°C), about 45 minutes longer. Alternatively, pierce
the thigh joint with the tip of a knife; the juices should run clear.

❀ Transfer the chicken to a cutting board and tent loosely with aluminum foil. Skim off and discard the fat from the pan drippings. Pour
the remaining ⅔ cup (5 fl oz/160 ml) broth into the pan and place on the
stove top over medium heat. Deglaze the pan, stirring with a whisk to
dislodge any browned bits from the pan bottom. Gradually whisk in the
¼ cup (2 fl oz/60 ml) cream. Continue to whisk until the sauce thickens,
about 2 minutes. If too thick, thin with additional broth or cream.

❀ Transfer the chicken to a warmed platter. Garnish with the remaining rosemary sprigs. Cut the remaining lemon into slices and arrange
around the chicken. Pour the sauce into a warmed bowl and pass at
the table.

NUTRITIONAL ANALYSIS PER SERVING: Calories 591 (Kilojoules 2,482); Protein 54 g;
Carbohydrates 5 g; Total Fat 39 g; Saturated Fat 12 g; Cholesterol 188 mg; Sodium 354 mg;
Dietary Fiber 1 g

Fettuccine with Brie and Asparagus

PREP TIME: 20 MINUTES

COOKING TIME: 10 MINUTES
IF USING FRESH PASTA,
20 MINUTES IF USING
DRIED PASTA

INGREDIENTS

1 lb (500 g) asparagus spears

3 tablespoons unsalted butter

½ cup (2 oz/60 g) unsalted pistachios,
coarsely chopped

4 teaspoons grated lemon zest

1 lb (500 g) fresh or dried fettuccine

½ lb (250 g) Brie cheese, rind
trimmed and cheese broken into
small pieces

½ cup (2 oz/60 g) grated Parmesan
cheese, preferably Parmigiano-
Reggiano

salt and ground pepper to taste

3 tablespoons chopped fresh flat-leaf
(Italian) parsley

When small pieces of Brie are tossed with warm strands of fettuccine, the cheese melts and forms a delectable sauce. Sautéed thinly sliced asparagus and chopped pistachio nuts add vivid color and texture to the dish. Sophisticated yet simple, this pasta goes together quickly after a day spent browsing flea markets or touring the local museums.

SERVES 4

❀ Fill a large pot three-fourths full of salted water and bring to a boil.

❀ While the water is heating, prepare the asparagus. Snap off the tough ends where they break naturally and discard. Starting at the base, slice the spears crosswise ⅛ inch (3 mm) thick, leaving the tips whole.

❀ In a large, heavy frying pan over medium-high heat, melt the butter. When hot, add the asparagus and cook, stirring constantly, until just tender, about 3 minutes. Remove from the heat and stir in the pistachios and lemon zest. Keep warm.

❀ Add the pasta to the boiling water and cook until al dente (tender, yet still firm to the bite), 2–3 minutes for fresh pasta and about 12 minutes or according to the package directions for dried pasta. Drain, reserving ⅓ cup (3 fl oz/80 ml) of the pasta cooking water, and return the pasta to the pot.

❀ Immediately add the Brie and Parmesan cheeses and the reserved asparagus mixture. Stir and toss well to combine the melting cheeses with the pasta. Add the reserved cooking water to the pasta as needed to moisten. Season with salt and pepper.

❀ Transfer the pasta to a warmed large serving bowl and sprinkle with the parsley. Serve at once.

NUTRITIONAL ANALYSIS PER SERVING: Calories 752 (Kilojoules 3,158); Protein 35 g; Carbohydrates 70 g; Total Fat 38 g; Saturated Fat 10 g; Cholesterol 175 mg; Sodium 482 mg; Dietary Fiber 5 g

Couscous with a Vegetable Mélange

PREP TIME: 50 MINUTES

COOKING TIME: 1 HOUR

INGREDIENTS

FOR THE FLAVORED STOCK

8 cups (64 fl oz/2 l) chicken broth

4 large plum (Roma) tomatoes, about ¾ lb (375 g) total weight, quartered lengthwise and seeded

1 yellow onion, cut lengthwise into 8 wedges

3 fresh flat-leaf (Italian) parsley sprigs

1 cinnamon stick, 3–4 inches (7.5–10 cm) long, broken in half

1 teaspoon ground black pepper

¼ teaspoon ground turmeric

¼ teaspoon red pepper flakes

2 carrots, peeled and sliced ½ inch (12 mm) thick

1 turnip, peeled and cut into ½-inch (12-mm) dice

1 small butternut squash, ¾–1 lb (375–500 g), halved, seeded, peeled, and cut into 1-inch (2.5-cm) dice

2 small zucchini (courgettes), trimmed and sliced ½ inch (12 mm) thick

1 red bell pepper (capsicum), seeded and cut into 1-inch (2.5-cm) squares

2 cups (10 oz/315 g) instant couscous

2 tablespoons unsalted butter

2 tablespoons chopped fresh flat-leaf (Italian) parsley

Both assertive and subtle flavors come together here to make an appealing dish that can stand alone as a main course for vegetarians (use vegetable broth in place of the chicken broth) or be served as a side dish to roast chicken or lamb. Enlist a willing guest to chop the vegetables while you prepare the stock.

SERVES 6

❀ To make the flavored stock, in a large, deep-sided saucepan over medium-high heat, combine the broth, tomatoes, onion, parsley sprigs, cinnamon stick, black pepper, turmeric, and red pepper flakes. Bring to a simmer, reduce the heat to low, cover, and cook until the flavors are blended, about 25 minutes. Remove from the heat and pour through a fine-mesh sieve into a large bowl, then return to the pan.

❀ Bring the stock to a simmer over medium heat. Add the carrots, turnip, and butternut squash. Cook, uncovered, until the vegetables are just tender, about 15 minutes. Add the zucchini and bell pepper and cook, uncovered, until just tender, 5–8 minutes longer. Using a slotted spoon, transfer the vegetables to a bowl and cover loosely with aluminum foil to keep warm.

❀ Pour off all but 3 cups (24 fl oz/750 ml) of the cooking liquid in the pan and set aside. Bring the liquid remaining in the pan to a boil, remove from the heat, and stir in the couscous and butter. Cover and let stand for 5 minutes.

❀ To serve, mound the couscous on a warmed serving platter. Arrange the vegetables on top and drizzle with ½ cup (4 fl oz/125 ml) of the reserved stock. Sprinkle the parsley over the top. Pour the remaining stock into a serving bowl and pass at the table.

NUTRITIONAL ANALYSIS PER SERVING: Calories 306 (Kilojoules 1,285); Protein 10 g; Carbohydrates 55 g; Total Fat 6 g; Saturated Fat 3 g; Cholesterol 10 mg; Sodium 704 mg; Dietary Fiber 5 g

Orange-Ginger Pork Tenderloins

PREP TIME: 35 MINUTES,
PLUS 6 HOURS FOR
MARINATING PORK

COOKING TIME: 30 MINUTES,
PLUS PREPARING FIRE

INGREDIENTS

2 pork tenderloins, about 1 lb (500 g) each, trimmed of fat

½ cup (4 fl oz/125 ml) thawed frozen orange juice concentrate

4 teaspoons soy sauce

1 tablespoon dry sherry

1 teaspoon Asian sesame oil

2 teaspoons peeled and grated fresh ginger

1 teaspoon minced garlic

1 teaspoon dried thyme

FOR THE GLAZE

¼ cup (2 fl oz/60 ml) thawed frozen orange juice concentrate

2 tablespoons molasses

2 teaspoons peeled and grated fresh ginger

¼ teaspoon dried thyme

¼ teaspoon ground pepper

salt to taste

1 orange, cut into 6 wedges

fresh thyme sprigs (optional)

Serve these tender, succulent pork slices with sesame-scented coleslaw and green beans for a warm-weather meal under the stars. Use any leftovers for sandwiches such as the pita pockets on page 56.

SERVES 6

❋ Pat the tenderloins dry. Place in a shallow nonaluminum dish or lock-top plastic bag. In a small bowl, stir together the ½ cup (4 fl oz/125 ml) orange juice concentrate, soy sauce, sherry, sesame oil, ginger, garlic, and thyme. Pour over the pork and cover the dish or seal the bag. Refrigerate for at least 6 hours or for as long as overnight, turning the meat occasionally. Bring to room temperature before cooking.

❋ Prepare a medium-hot fire in a charcoal grill.

❋ To make the glaze, in a small bowl, stir together the ¼ cup (2 fl oz/ 60 ml) orange juice concentrate, molasses, ginger, thyme, and pepper. Set aside.

❋ Remove the tenderloins from the marinade and place on the grill rack 4–5 inches (10–13 cm) above the fire. Grill, turning frequently, for 15 minutes. Then brush generously with some of the glaze and continue grilling, basting frequently, until an instant-read thermometer inserted into the thickest part of the meat registers 150°F (65°C), about 15 minutes longer. Watch carefully. The cooking time will vary depending upon the type of grill and the intensity of the heat. The meat should have a rosy hue at the center when cut into with a sharp knife.

❋ Transfer to a cutting board, tent with aluminum foil, and let rest for 10 minutes. To serve, cut the tenderloins crosswise on a sharp diagonal into slices ¼ inch (6 mm) thick. Arrange the slices, overlapping them, on a serving plate, season lightly with salt, and brush with any remaining glaze. Garnish with the orange wedges and thyme sprigs, if using.

NUTRITIONAL ANALYSIS PER SERVING: Calories 271 (Kilojoules 1,138); Protein 31 g; Carbohydrates 20 g; Total Fat 7 g; Saturated Fat 2 g; Cholesterol 92 mg; Sodium 239 mg; Dietary Fiber 1 g

Honey and Jalapeño Grilled Salmon

PREP TIME: 30 MINUTES,
    PLUS 2 HOURS FOR
    MARINATING SALMON

COOKING TIME: 25 MINUTES,
    PLUS PREPARING FIRE

INGREDIENTS

6 salmon fillets with skin intact,
    6–7 oz (185–220 g) each

½ cup (4 fl oz/125 ml) lime juice

3 tablespoons olive oil

4–5 teaspoons minced jalapeño chile

2 teaspoons minced garlic

1 teaspoon grated lime zest

¼ cup (3 oz/90 g) honey

2 limes

salt to taste

SERVING TIP: If you have any salmon
and glaze left over, break the fish into
chunks and combine with mixed salad
greens and crumbled feta. Drizzle
with the glaze for a light dressing.

The sweetness of honey, the spiciness of jalapeño chiles, and
the tartness of lime complement salmon deliciously. Serve with
a pitcher of ice-cold margaritas for a south-of-the-border-
inspired evening.

SERVES 6

❀ Check the fillets and remove any errant bones. Place the fish in a
shallow nonaluminum dish. In a small bowl, stir together the lime
juice, olive oil, 2 teaspoons of the minced jalapeño, the garlic, and the
lime zest. Pour over the salmon and turn to coat well. Cover with plastic
wrap and refrigerate for 2 hours, turning occasionally. Bring to room
temperature 30 minutes before cooking.

❀ Prepare a medium-hot fire in a charcoal grill.

❀ Remove the salmon from the marinade, and pour the marinade into
a small saucepan. Place over high heat, bring to a boil, and boil until
reduced by half. Stir in the honey and set aside to use as a glaze.

❀ Place the salmon, flesh side down, on the oiled grill rack and grill,
turning once, until the fish is opaque throughout, 6–7 minutes on
each side.

❀ While the salmon is cooking, remove the zest from the 2 limes in
long, narrow strips, then cut the limes in half.

❀ When the salmon is done, transfer to a serving platter. Season each
fillet with salt and squeeze some lime juice from the halved limes over
each. Brush each fillet generously with the glaze, and sprinkle the lime
zest and the remaining 2–3 teaspoons jalapeño evenly over the salmon.
Serve immediately.

NUTRITIONAL ANALYSIS PER SERVING: Calories 451 (Kilojoules 1,894); Protein 37 g;
Carbohydrates 15 g; Total Fat 27 g; Saturated Fat 5 g; Cholesterol 109 mg; Sodium 113 mg;
Dietary Fiber 0 g

Grilled Flank Steak with Horseradish Mashed Potatoes

PREP TIME: 30 MINUTES, PLUS
2 HOURS FOR MARINATING
STEAK

COOKING TIME: 25 MINUTES,
PLUS PREPARING FIRE

INGREDIENTS

1 flank steak, 1½ lb (750 g), trimmed
of fat

6 cloves garlic, finely chopped

2 tablespoons red wine vinegar

1 tablespoon olive oil

2 teaspoons dried thyme

FOR THE POTATOES

2 lb (1 kg) Yukon gold potatoes,
peeled and cut into 1-inch (2.5-cm)
cubes

⅔ cup (2½ oz/75 g) shredded
Gruyère cheese

½ cup (4 fl oz/125 ml) milk, or as
needed, heated

3–3½ tablespoons prepared
horseradish

1½ tablespoons unsalted butter,
at room temperature

1½ teaspoons Dijon mustard

½ teaspoon salt

scant ½ teaspoon ground pepper

salt and ground pepper to taste

fresh thyme sprigs (optional)

1 tablespoon chopped fresh flat-leaf
(Italian) parsley

Flank steak has a rich flavor and is relatively inexpensive. That means you can serve a tasty steak dinner to your friends without breaking the bank. Ask one of your guests to supervise the grilling while you make the mashed potatoes.

SERVES 4

❀ Place the steak in a shallow nonaluminum dish. In a small bowl, stir together the garlic, vinegar, olive oil, and thyme. Brush the mixture on both sides of the steak, cover, and refrigerate for at least 2 hours or for up to 24 hours. Bring to room temperature before cooking.

❀ Prepare a fire in a charcoal grill.

❀ To make the mashed potatoes, bring a saucepan three-fourths full of lightly salted water to a boil. Add the potatoes and cook until easily pierced with a sharp knife, about 15 minutes. Drain well and place in a bowl. Add the cheese, ½ cup (4 fl oz/125 ml) milk, 3 tablespoons horseradish, butter, mustard, ½ teaspoon salt, and scant ½ teaspoon pepper. Using an electric mixer set on low speed, beat only until the ingredients are incorporated. Taste and add additional horseradish, if needed, then taste again and adjust the seasonings. If the potatoes are too thick, thin by beating in a small amount of additional warm milk. Cover loosely with aluminum foil until serving.

❀ Just before the potatoes are ready to drain, put the steak on the oiled grill rack 4–5 inches (10–13 cm) above the fire. Grill, turning once, for 4–5 minutes on each side. (Alternatively, cook the steak in a broiler/griller using the same timing.) Transfer the steak to a cutting board, and sprinkle generously with salt and pepper. Let rest for 5 minutes.

❀ To serve, thinly slice the meat against the grain. Arrange the slices, overlapping them, on a warmed platter along with the mashed potatoes. Garnish the meat with the thyme sprigs, if using, and sprinkle the potatoes with the parsley. Serve at once.

NUTRITIONAL ANALYSIS PER SERVING: Calories 532 (Kilojoules 2,234); Protein 36 g; Carbohydrates 42 g; Total Fat 24 g; Saturated Fat 11 g; Cholesterol 97 mg; Sodium 515 mg; Dietary Fiber 4 g

Seafood Stew with Tomatoes, Shrimp, and Scallops

PREP TIME: 45 MINUTES

COOKING TIME: 25 MINUTES

INGREDIENTS

¼ cup (2 fl oz/60 ml) olive oil

2 yellow onions, chopped (about
1½ cups/6 oz/185 g)

4 small carrots, peeled and cut into
¼-inch (6-mm) dice (about 1 cup/
5 oz/155 g)

2 teaspoons chopped garlic

2 cans (28 oz/875 g each) plum
(Roma) tomatoes, drained and cut
into ½-inch (12-mm) dice

3 cups (24 fl oz/750 ml) chicken
broth

⅔ cup (5 fl oz/160 ml) dry white
wine

2 tablespoons chopped fresh basil

2 teaspoons grated orange zest

½ teaspoon red pepper flakes

½ teaspoon salt

1 lb (500 g) Chilean sea bass,
halibut, or other firm-fleshed
whitefish fillet, skinned and cut
into 1–1½-inch (2.5–4-cm) cubes

¾ lb (375 g) sea scallops

¾ lb (375 g) large shrimp (prawns),
peeled and deveined

2 tablespoons julienned fresh basil
leaves

6 orange wedges, each ½ inch
(12 mm) thick

Here is a satisfying seafood stew for a Saturday night supper during a weekend spent at the beach. Let the best of the day's catch at your local seafood market determine the recipe's final ingredients. Salad fixings from a local farmers' market and a loaf of bread from your favorite bakery are all you need to complete the meal.

SERVES 6

✱ In a large, heavy saucepan over medium heat, warm the olive oil. When hot, add the onions and carrots and sauté, stirring occasionally, until slightly softened, about 4 minutes. Add the garlic and cook for 1 minute, until fragrant. Add the tomatoes, broth, wine, basil, orange zest, red pepper flakes, and salt. Bring to a simmer, reduce the heat to low, and cook, uncovered, for about 10 minutes to blend the flavors.

✱ Add the fish cubes and simmer for about 3 minutes. Add the scallops and shrimp and continue to simmer until the fish and scallops are opaque throughout and the shrimp are curled and pink, 2–3 minutes longer. Taste and adjust the seasonings.

✱ Ladle into warmed shallow soup bowls. Sprinkle each serving with about 1 teaspoon julienned basil leaves and place an orange wedge alongside. Each diner should squeeze the juice from the orange wedge into the stew before eating.

NUTRITIONAL ANALYSIS PER SERVING: Calories 375 (Kilojoules 1,575); Protein 37 g; Carbohydrates 23 g; Total Fat 14 g; Saturated Fat 2 g; Cholesterol 120 mg; Sodium 1,347 mg; Dietary Fiber 4 g

Pepper-and-Cumin-Coated Lamb Chops

PREP TIME: 15 MINUTES,
PLUS 30 MINUTES FOR
MARINATING

COOKING TIME: 20 MINUTES

INGREDIENTS

1½ tablespoons cumin seeds

1 tablespoon coarsely ground pepper

1½ teaspoons kosher salt

18 rib lamb chops, about 4 oz
   (125 g) each, trimmed of fat

2–3 teaspoons olive oil

fresh mint sprigs (optional)

COOKING TIP: If you do not have a stove-top grill pan, use a large frying pan and cover the bottom with a thin film of olive oil. Heat until the oil is hot and then add the chops.

A dry rub of just three ingredients—coarsely ground pepper, cumin, and salt—adds hearty flavor to lamb. Cooked on a stove-top grill pan, these chops are a quick and easy main course; yet they're special enough for a celebratory meal on a Saturday night. Serve with Couscous with a Vegetable Mélange (page 66).

SERVES 6

❋ Place the cumin seeds in a small lock-top plastic bag and crush coarsely using a meat pounder or rolling pin. Place the crushed seeds in a small bowl and add the pepper and kosher salt. Mix well.

❋ Pat the chops dry, then pat ¼ teaspoon of seasoning mixture on each side of each chop. Place the chops on a baking sheet, cover with aluminum foil, and refrigerate for 30 minutes.

❋ When ready to cook, brush a stove-top grill pan lightly with olive oil and place over medium heat. When hot, add enough chops to fit comfortably in a single layer and cook on one side until brown and crusty, about 3 minutes. Turn and cook until brown and crusty on the second side but still pink in the center when cut into with a sharp knife, about 3 minutes longer. Transfer to a warmed platter and cover loosely with aluminum foil. Repeat with the remaining chops until all are cooked, brushing the pan with more oil as needed to prevent sticking.

❋ Garnish with a small bouquet of fresh mint, if desired. Serve at once.

NUTRITIONAL ANALYSIS PER SERVING: Calories 301 (Kilojoules 1,264); Protein 32 g; Carbohydrates 1 g; Total Fat 18 g; Saturated Fat 6 g; Cholesterol 105 mg; Sodium 467 mg; Dietary Fiber 0 g

Texas-Style Chili

PREP TIME: 45 MINUTES

COOKING TIME: 3 HOURS

INGREDIENTS

FOR THE CHILI

3 lb (1.5 kg) lean beef stew meat

about 3 tablespoons vegetable oil

2 carrots, peeled and finely diced

2 yellow onions, chopped

4 teaspoons chopped garlic

3 tablespoons all-purpose (plain) flour

¼ cup (2 oz/60 g) chili powder

3½ teaspoons ground cumin

2¼ teaspoons dried oregano

1½ teaspoons salt

¼ teaspoon red pepper flakes

2 cans (28 oz/875 g each) plum (Roma) tomatoes, drained and chopped

5–6 cups (40–48 fl oz/1.25–1.5 l) reduced-sodium beef broth

2 chipotle chiles

FOR BEANS AND GARNISH

2 cans (15 oz/470 g each) black beans

2 teaspoons vegetable oil

1 small yellow onion, chopped

1 cup (4 oz/125 g) shredded Monterey jack cheese

1 cup (8 fl oz/250 ml) sour cream

2 tablespoons chopped fresh cilantro (fresh coriander)

On a weekend when friends have gathered to watch the big game, offer bowls of this pleasantly spicy chili along with plenty of ice-cold beer and homemade corn bread.

SERVES 6

❋ To make the chili, trim away all the fat from the beef, then cut into ¾-inch (2-cm) cubes and pat dry. In a large, heavy, deep-sided pot, pour in enough vegetable oil to form a film on the bottom; place over medium heat. When hot, add the meat, in batches, in a single layer. Cook, turning often, until browned on all sides, 3–5 minutes. Transfer to a plate and repeat until all the meat is browned, adding more oil as needed.

❋ Add more oil to the pot to coat the bottom and place over medium heat. Add the carrots, onions, and garlic and cook, stirring, until the vegetables are slightly softened, about 2 minutes. Return the browned meat to the pot and sprinkle the meat and vegetables with the flour. Cook, stirring vigorously, for 1 minute. Add the chili powder, cumin, oregano, salt, red pepper flakes, tomatoes, 5 cups (40 fl oz/1.25 l) broth, and chipotle chiles. Bring to a simmer, then reduce the heat to low, cover, and cook for about 30 minutes. Uncover and continue to cook, stirring occasionally, until the meat is fork tender, 1½–2 hours longer. If the chili becomes too thick, thin with as much of the remaining 1 cup (8 fl oz/250 ml) beef broth as needed. Taste and adjust the seasonings. Remove and discard the chipotle chiles.

❋ To prepare the beans, rinse and drain them, then pat dry. In a large, heavy frying pan over medium-high heat, warm the vegetable oil. When hot, add the onion and cook, stirring often, until softened, about 3 minutes. Add the beans and cook, stirring, until hot, 2–3 minutes longer. Divide the beans among shallow soup bowls and ladle the chili over them. Garnish each serving with the jack cheese, a generous dollop of sour cream, and a sprinkling of cilantro.

NUTRITIONAL ANALYSIS PER SERVING: Calories 770 (Kilojoules 3,234); Protein 69 g; Carbohydrates 46 g; Total Fat 36 g; Saturated Fat 13 g; Cholesterol 173 mg; Sodium 2,192 mg; Dietary Fiber 12 g

Lasagne with Spinach, Prosciutto, and Herbed Ricotta

PREP TIME: 30 MINUTES

COOKING TIME: 1¼ HOURS

INGREDIENTS

about 5 tablespoons (2½ oz/75 ml)
olive oil

1½ lb (750 g) baby or flat-leaf
spinach, tough stems removed

½ cup (2 oz/60 g) chopped shallot

¾ lb (375 g) fresh portobello
mushrooms, brushed clean and
coarsely chopped

¼ lb (125 g) sliced prosciutto,
coarsely chopped

½ teaspoon salt

2¼ cups (18 oz/560 g) ricotta cheese

1¾ cups (7 oz/215 g) grated
Parmesan cheese, preferably
Parmigiano-Reggiano

½ cup (¾ oz/20 g) chopped fresh
flat-leaf (Italian) parsley

¼ teaspoon ground nutmeg

1 egg yolk

¾ lb (375 g) fresh pasta sheets, cut
into 2½-by-10-inch (6-by-25-cm)
strips, or dried lasagne noodles

1½ cups (6 oz/185 g) shredded
fontina cheese, preferably Italian
Fontina Val d'Aosta

MAKE-AHEAD TIP: Assemble the
lasagne, cover, and refrigerate for up
to 4 hours before baking. Increase
the baking time by 5–10 minutes.

Prepare this dish ahead of time and pop it in the oven when your
guests arrive. By the time they've settled in, it will be ready to serve.

SERVES 8

❀ Preheat an oven to 400°F (200°C). Oil a 3-qt (3-l) flameproof baking
dish such as a 9-by-13-inch (23-by-33-cm) dish with 2-inch (5-cm) sides.

❀ In a large frying pan over medium heat, pour in enough of the olive
oil to form a film on the bottom. When hot, add some of the spinach
and toss until wilted, 3–4 minutes. Using tongs, transfer to a colander.
Repeat, adding oil if necessary, until all the spinach is wilted. Let cool.

❀ Wipe out the frying pan. Pour in 3 tablespoons of the olive oil and
place over medium-high heat. Add the shallot and mushrooms and sauté
until softened, about 3 minutes. Stir in the prosciutto and remove from
the heat. Press out as much liquid as possible from the spinach, then
stir it into the mushroom mixture. Add the salt and set aside.

❀ In a bowl, combine the ricotta cheese, 1½ cups (6 oz/185 g) of the
Parmesan cheese, all but 2 teaspoons of the parsley, the nutmeg, and
the egg yolk. Mix well. Set aside.

❀ Bring a large pot three-fourths full of salted water to a boil. Add the
pasta and cook until al dente (tender, yet still firm to the bite), 3–4 minutes if using fresh pasta and 12 minutes if using dried. Drain, transfer
to a bowl of cold water until cool, then lay flat on kitchen towels to drain.

❀ Using about one-third of the pasta, arrange a layer of noodles, slightly
overlapping, in the prepared dish. Cover with half of the ricotta mixture,
then with half of the spinach mixture, and finally with ½ cup (2 oz/60 g)
of the fontina. Repeat the layers, then top with the remaining noodles.

❀ Cover with aluminum foil and bake until bubbling and hot, 35–40 minutes. Remove from the oven, uncover, and sprinkle with the remaining
¼ cup (1 oz/30 g) Parmesan and ½ cup (2 oz/60 g) fontina.

❀ Turn on the broiler (griller). Slip the baking dish under the broiler
5–6 inches (13–15 cm) from the heat source and broil (grill) until golden,
about 5 minutes. Remove from the broiler and let stand for 10 minutes.
Sprinkle with the reserved 2 teaspoons parsley and serve.

NUTRITIONAL ANALYSIS PER SERVING: Calories 563 (Kilojoules 2,365); Protein 33 g;
Carbohydrates 31 g; Total Fat 35 g; Saturated Fat 17 g; Cholesterol 148 mg; Sodium 852 mg;
Dietary Fiber 3 g

Skewers of Swordfish, Red Peppers, and Oranges

PREP TIME: 40 MINUTES,
PLUS 1½ HOURS FOR
MARINATING FISH

COOKING TIME: 10 MINUTES,
PLUS PREPARING FIRE

INGREDIENTS

1⅓ lb (21 oz/655 g) swordfish steaks, about 1 inch (2.5 cm) thick, boned, skinned, and cut into 1-inch (2.5-cm) cubes

5 thick-skinned navel oranges

¼ cup (2 fl oz/60 ml) olive oil

1 tablespoon white balsamic vinegar or white wine vinegar

¼ teaspoon plus ⅛ teaspoon salt, plus salt to taste

¼ teaspoon ground pepper

6 tablespoons (½ oz/15 g) julienned fresh basil leaves, plus several sprigs for garnish

¼ cup (2 oz/60 g) unsalted butter, at room temperature

2 red bell peppers (capsicums), seeded and cut into 1-inch (2.5-cm) squares

COOKING TIP: The skewers can instead be cooked in a broiler (griller) using the same timing.

Serve these colorful skewers for an outdoor buffet. Accompany them with basmati rice or couscous and sautéed fennel or zucchini (courgettes).

SERVES 4

❀ Place the swordfish cubes in a shallow nonaluminum dish. Set aside.

❀ Grate the zest from 2 oranges, then juice them. Place the zest and juice in a small bowl and add the olive oil, vinegar, the ¼ teaspoon salt, ⅛ teaspoon of the pepper, and 3 tablespoons of the basil. Whisk well and pour over the swordfish. Turn the fish to coat evenly, cover with plastic wrap, and refrigerate, turning several times, for 1½–2 hours.

❀ Cut 2 of the remaining oranges lengthwise into 8 neat wedges each. Cut each wedge in half crosswise and set aside.

❀ Grate enough zest from the remaining orange to measure 2 teaspoons and place the zest in a small bowl. Juice the orange and add 1 tablespoon of the juice to the bowl; reserve the remaining juice. Add to the bowl the remaining 3 tablespoons basil, ⅛ teaspoon each salt and pepper, and the butter and mix well. Cover and let stand at cool room temperature while the fish is marinating.

❀ If using wooden skewers, soak in water to cover for 30 minutes. Prepare a fire in a charcoal grill. Thread the bell pepper squares onto the skewers alternately with the orange wedges and swordfish cubes. Place the skewers on a long tray or rimmed baking sheet and pour any marinade remaining in the dish over the top.

❀ Place the skewers on an oiled grill rack 4–5 inches (10–13 cm) above the fire. Grill, turning once and basting with the seasoned butter, until the fish is opaque throughout, 4–5 minutes on each side.

❀ Transfer the skewers to a platter and season with salt. Drizzle as much of the reserved orange juice over the top as desired and garnish with basil sprigs. Serve at once.

NUTRITIONAL ANALYSIS PER SERVING: Calories 465 (Kilojoules 1,953); Protein 28 g; Carbohydrates 20 g; Total Fat 31 g; Saturated Fat 11 g; Cholesterol 83 mg; Sodium 345 mg; Dietary Fiber 3 g

Pappardelle with Chicken, Caramelized Onions, and Rosemary

PREP TIME: 40 MINUTES

COOKING TIME: 1½ HOURS

INGREDIENTS

about 6½ tablespoons (3½ fl oz/ 105 ml) olive oil, plus extra if needed

4½ cups (1 lb/500 g) thinly sliced yellow onion (3 or 4 onions)

½ teaspoon sugar

2½ lb (1.25 kg) boneless, skinless chicken breasts, trimmed of fat and cut into 1-inch (2.5-cm) cubes

1 tablespoon chopped garlic

3 tablespoons all-purpose (plain) flour

3 tablespoons finely chopped fresh rosemary

½ teaspoon salt, plus salt to taste

¼ teaspoon ground pepper

3 cups (24 fl oz/750 ml) reduced-sodium chicken broth

1 cup (8 fl oz/250 ml) dry white wine

3 fresh parsley sprigs, preferably flat-leaf (Italian), plus ½ cup (¾ oz/20 g) chopped parsley

1¼ lb (625 g) fresh pappardelle or fresh pasta sheets cut into noodles 12 inches (30 cm) long and ⅝ inch (1.5 cm) wide, preferably with a fluted pastry cutter

1 tablespoon unsalted butter

6 oz (185 g) fresh, creamy goat cheese, broken into small pieces

1 tablespoon grated lemon zest

You can use fresh or dried pappardelle or fettuccine with excellent results. The combination of crumbled goat cheese, lemon zest, and herbs makes a particularly pleasing garnish.

SERVES 6

✺ In a large, heavy, deep-sided pot over medium heat, warm 2 tablespoons of the olive oil. When hot, add the onions and sugar and cook, stirring constantly, until the onions are limp and golden brown, about 15 minutes. Transfer to a plate.

✺ Add 2 tablespoons of the oil to the same pot and place over medium-high heat. Working in batches, add only enough chicken to make a single layer and cook, turning often, until browned, 2–3 minutes or longer. Using a slotted utensil, transfer to a plate and repeat until all the chicken is browned, adding more oil as needed.

✺ Return all the browned chicken to the pot and place over medium-high heat. Add the garlic and stir for a minute until fragrant. Sprinkle the chicken with the flour and toss well. Add 2½ tablespoons of the rosemary, the ½ teaspoon salt, and the pepper and stir to combine. Stir in the broth, wine, parsley sprigs, and the reserved onions and bring to a simmer. Reduce the heat to low and cook, uncovered, until the chicken is fork tender, about 45 minutes. Taste and adjust the seasonings. Remove and discard the parsley sprigs.

✺ Just before the chicken is ready, bring a large pot three-fourths full of salted water to a boil. Add the pasta, stir well, and cook until al dente (tender, yet still firm to the bite), about 3 minutes. Drain and return to the pot. Add the butter and salt to taste and toss well.

✺ To serve, divide the pasta among warmed individual plates and ladle the chicken-onion mixture on top, dividing evenly. Sprinkle each serving with equal amounts of the goat cheese, lemon zest, chopped parsley, and the remaining ½ tablespoon rosemary. Serve immediately.

NUTRITIONAL ANALYSIS PER SERVING: Calories 764 (Kilojoules 3,209); Protein 62 g; Carbohydrates 63 g; Total Fat 27 g; Saturated Fat 8 g; Cholesterol 197 mg; Sodium 732 mg; Dietary Fiber 4 g

Pizza with Tomatoes, Olives, and Pancetta

PREP TIME: 45 MINUTES,
PLUS 45 MINUTES FOR
DOUGH TO RISE

COOKING TIME: 15 MINUTES

INGREDIENTS

FOR THE DOUGH

1½ cups (7½ oz/235 g) all-purpose (plain) flour, plus up to 1 tablespoon, if needed

2½ teaspoons (1 envelope) quick-rise active dry yeast

½ teaspoon salt

½ teaspoon sugar

½ cup (4 fl oz/125 ml) warm water (115°–125°F/46°–52°C), plus up to 1 tablespoon, if needed

1 tablespoon olive oil

FOR THE TOPPING

12–16 thin pancetta slices

10 plum (Roma) tomatoes, halved, seeded, and cut into wedges

2 teaspoons balsamic vinegar

2 generous pinches red pepper flakes

6 oz (185 g) fresh, creamy goat cheese

30 Kalamata olives, pitted and sliced

1 teaspoon dried basil

1 teaspoon dried oregano

1 cup (4 oz/125 g) shredded fontina cheese

about ¼ cup (2 fl oz/60 ml) extra-virgin olive oil

¼ cup (½ oz/15 g) julienned fresh basil leaves

Invite guests into the kitchen to help you make this delicious pizza. They'll enjoy shaping the dough and helping prepare the toppings.

SERVES 4–6

❋ To make the dough, in a food processor, combine the 1½ cups (7½ oz/235 g) flour, yeast, salt, and sugar. Process briefly to mix. With the motor running, pour in ½ cup (4 fl oz/125 ml) warm water and the olive oil in a steady stream, processing until the dough forms a ball. If it seems too wet, add up to 1 tablespoon flour; if too dry, add up to 1 tablespoon water. Transfer to a lightly floured work surface and knead a few times to form a smooth ball. Place the dough in an oiled mixing bowl, cover, and let rise in a warm place until almost doubled in bulk, 45–60 minutes.

❋ Position oven racks in the middle and lower third of an oven and preheat to 450°F (230°C). Lightly grease 2 baking sheets.

❋ Punch down the dough and divide in half. On a lightly floured work surface, roll out each half into a very thin 12-inch (30-cm) round. Fold over the outer ½-inch (12-mm) edge of each round and pinch to make a rim. Prick the rounds all over with the tines of a fork and place on the prepared baking sheets. (If desired, cover with plastic wrap, and then with aluminum foil, and refrigerate for up to 1 day. Bring to room temperature for 30 minutes before baking.)

❋ To make the topping, in a large frying pan over medium-low heat, cook the pancetta slices, turning occasionally, until crisp, 5–6 minutes. Transfer to paper towels to drain. When cool, crumble and set aside. In a bowl, toss together the tomatoes, vinegar, and red pepper flakes.

❋ Bake the pizza crusts for 5 minutes to crisp slightly, then remove from the oven. Spread each warm crust with half of the goat cheese, then top each with half of the tomato mixture. Sprinkle each pizza with half each of the olives, pancetta, dried basil, oregano, and fontina cheese. Drizzle each with 1½–2 tablespoons olive oil.

❋ Bake until the cheese melts and the crusts are crisp, 5–8 minutes. Remove from the oven and sprinkle each pizza with 2 tablespoons of the fresh basil. Cut each pizza into 6 wedges and serve immediately.

NUTRITIONAL ANALYSIS PER SERVING: Calories 590 (Kilojoules 2,477); Protein 19 g; Carbohydrates 36 g; Total Fat 41 g; Saturated Fat 14 g; Cholesterol 52 mg; Sodium 1,203 mg; Dietary Fiber 2 g

Compote of Strawberries and Raspberries in Red Wine Sauce

PREP TIME: 25 MINUTES, PLUS
1 HOUR FOR THICKENING
CRÈME FRAÎCHE

COOKING TIME: 30 MINUTES

INGREDIENTS

FOR THE QUICK CRÈME FRAÎCHE

⅔ cup (5 fl oz/160 ml) sour cream

⅓ cup (3 fl oz/80 ml) half-and-half
(half cream)

FOR THE SAUCE

2 cups (16 fl oz/500 ml) water

1 cup (8 fl oz/250 ml) dry red wine

1 cup (8 oz/250 g) sugar

1 teaspoon ground cinnamon

⅛ teaspoon ground cloves

2¼ cups (10 oz/315 g) raspberries

2¼ cups (9 oz/280 g) strawberries,
stemmed and halved

4 fresh mint sprigs

PREP TIP: Substitute pitted fresh cherries for all or part of the strawberries or raspberries, if you like.

When you're out for a country drive with summertime visitors, stop at a stand selling farm-fresh berries to stock up for this simply delicious dessert.

SERVES 4

❀ To make the quick crème fraîche, in a small bowl, whisk together the sour cream and half-and-half. Let stand at room temperature until thickened, 30–60 minutes. Cover and refrigerate until needed.

❀ Meanwhile, make the sauce: In a heavy saucepan over medium-high heat, combine the water, wine, sugar, cinnamon, and cloves. Bring to a simmer, stirring to dissolve the sugar and spices. Reduce the heat to low and simmer, uncovered, until the mixture becomes syrupy and has reduced to 1 cup (8 fl oz/250 ml), about 30 minutes. Remove from the heat. (If not using immediately, cool, cover, and refrigerate for up to 2 days. Reheat over low heat, stirring often, before using.)

❀ In a bowl, combine the raspberries and strawberries. Stir gently to mix, then divide evenly among shallow individual bowls. Pour ¼ cup (2 fl oz/60 ml) of the warm sauce over each serving, and top each with a generous dollop of crème fraîche. Garnish each serving with a mint sprig. Pass the remaining crème fraîche at the table.

NUTRITIONAL ANALYSIS PER SERVING: Calories 436 (Kilojoules 1,831); Protein 4 g; Carbohydrates 86 g; Total Fat 11 g; Saturated Fat 6 g; Cholesterol 23 mg; Sodium 31 mg; Dietary Fiber 5 g

Warm Plum Gratin

PREP TIME: 35 MINUTES

COOKING TIME: 40 MINUTES

INGREDIENTS

FOR THE PLUM MIXTURE

2 lb (1 kg) firm, slightly underripe plums, preferably Santa Rosa or other large, dark red or purple variety

5 tablespoons (2½ oz/75 g) firmly packed light brown sugar

3 tablespoons all-purpose (plain) flour

¾ teaspoon ground cinnamon

¼ teaspoon ground ginger

FOR THE STREUSEL TOPPING

6 tablespoons (2 oz/60 g) all-purpose (plain) flour

6 tablespoons (3 oz/90 g) firmly packed light brown sugar

¼ teaspoon ground cinnamon

⅔ cup (2½ oz/75 g) sliced (flaked) almonds

4½ tablespoons (2¼ oz/67 g) chilled unsalted butter, cut into small bits

6 fresh mint sprigs

PREP TIP: Plums vary in sweetness. After mixing the plums with the spices and sugar, taste to see if additional sugar is needed.

In this mouthwatering dessert gratin, a sweet almond streusel covers spice-dusted plums. Top each serving with a scoop of vanilla ice cream or a dollop of sour cream sweetened to taste with honey.

SERVES 6

❈ Preheat an oven to 375°F (190°C). Butter a shallow 2-qt (2-l) baking dish.

❈ To prepare the plums, halve and discard the pits. Cut each half into 4 wedges. In a large bowl, stir together the brown sugar, flour, cinnamon, and ginger. Add the plums and toss to coat well. Spread the plum mixture in the prepared baking dish.

❈ To make the streusel, in a bowl, using a fork, stir together the flour, brown sugar, and cinnamon. Add the almonds and butter. Using your fingertips, combine the ingredients to form uniform clumps. Pat the streusel mixture evenly on top of the plums.

❈ Bake until the top has browned, the juices are bubbling, and the plums are tender when pierced with a fork, about 40 minutes. When done, remove from the oven and let cool slightly.

❈ Spoon the warm gratin onto individual dessert plates and garnish each with a mint sprig.

NUTRITIONAL ANALYSIS PER SERVING: Calories 377 (Kilojoules 1,583); Protein 5 g; Carbohydrates 57 g; Total Fat 16 g; Saturated Fat 6 g; Cholesterol 25 mg; Sodium 13 mg; Dietary Fiber 4 g

Chocolate Pudding with Toffee Pecan Crumble

PREP TIME: 35 MINUTES

COOKING TIME: 45 MINUTES,
    PLUS 30 MINUTES FOR
    COOLING

INGREDIENTS

FOR THE PUDDING

2 cups (16 fl oz/500 ml) milk

½ cup (1½ oz/45 g) cocoa powder,
    preferably Dutch-process

4 whole eggs plus 3 egg yolks

1 cup (8 oz/250 g) granulated sugar

1½ teaspoons vanilla extract (essence)

FOR THE TOPPING

¾ cup (6 fl oz/180 ml) heavy (double)
    cream

2 tablespoons toffee bits

2 tablespoons coarsely chopped
    pecans

1 tablespoon light brown sugar

MAKE-AHEAD TIP: The pudding can
be made up to 1 day ahead. Let cool,
cover, and refrigerate, then bring to
room temperature before garnishing
and serving.

Here, a smooth, silky pudding and a crunchy sweet topping
combine for a wonderful match. Toffee bits, small morsels of
caramel-flavored candy, are available packaged in the baking
section of most food stores.

SERVES 6

❀ Preheat an oven to 325°F (165°C).

❀ To make the pudding, pour the milk into a heavy saucepan. Sift the
cocoa over the milk. Place the pan over medium heat and whisk constantly
until the cocoa dissolves and small bubbles appear along the edges of
the pan. Remove from the heat and set aside to cool for 5 minutes.

❀ In a bowl, using an electric mixer set on medium speed, beat together
the whole eggs and egg yolks until well combined.

❀ Gradually add the granulated sugar, continuing to beat until the mixture is slightly thickened and light in color, about 1 minute. Do not over-
beat. Reduce the speed to low and add the reserved milk mixture and
vanilla, beating only long enough to incorporate. Divide the mixture
evenly among six 1-cup (8–fl oz/250-ml) ramekins. Place the ramekins
in a heavy, shallow baking dish. Pour hot water into the baking dish to
reach halfway up the sides of the ramekins.

❀ Place the dish in the oven and bake until a knife inserted into the
center of a pudding comes out clean, 30–35 minutes. Transfer the
ramekins to a rack and let cool to room temperature, about 30 minutes.

❀ Just before serving, make the topping: In a chilled bowl, using an electric mixer or a whisk, beat the cream just until firm peaks form. In a
small bowl, stir together the toffee bits, pecans, and brown sugar. Place
the cream in dollops on top of each pudding, dividing evenly. Sprinkle
the puddings evenly with the toffee mixture and serve.

NUTRITIONAL ANALYSIS PER SERVING: Calories 450 (Kilojoules 1,890); Protein 10 g;
Carbohydrates 52 g; Total Fat 24 g; Saturated Fat 12 g; Cholesterol 302 mg; Sodium 177 mg;
Dietary Fiber 0 g

Warm Pear and Dried Cranberry Bread Pudding

PREP TIME: 1 HOUR, PLUS
4 HOURS FOR CHILLING

COOKING TIME: 1 HOUR

INGREDIENTS

7 tablespoons (3½ oz/105 g) unsalted butter

4 firm, full-flavored pears such as Anjou, peeled, quartered, cored, and cut into slices ⅛ inch (3 mm) thick

1 cup (7 oz/220 g) firmly packed light brown sugar

1 teaspoon ground cinnamon

3–4 loaves day-old French bread such as baguettes, each about 18 inches (45 cm) long, crusts removed and bread cut into ½-inch (12-mm) cubes (about 10 cups/ scant 2 lb/scant 1 kg)

¾ cup (3 oz/90 g) dried cranberries

6 eggs

1 teaspoon almond extract (essence)

¼ teaspoon ground nutmeg

scant ⅛ teaspoon salt

4 cups (32 fl oz/1 l) half-and-half (half cream)

MAKE-AHEAD TIP: The baked pudding can rest at room temperature for up to 2 hours. Reheat in a 350°F (180°C) oven until warm.

This is comfort food at its best. A scoop of vanilla ice cream or frozen yogurt makes a splendid partner.

SERVES 10

❀ Coat a 9-by-13-inch (23-by-33-cm) baking dish with 2-inch (5-cm) sides or similar 3-qt (3-l) baking dish with nonstick cooking spray.

❀ In a large, heavy frying pan over medium-high heat, melt 4 tablespoons (2 oz/60 g) of the butter. When hot, add the pear slices, ¼ cup (2 oz/60 g) of the brown sugar, and the cinnamon and sauté, stirring constantly, until the pears are softened, about 8 minutes. Remove from the heat and set aside.

❀ In a small saucepan over low heat, melt the remaining 3 tablespoons butter. Spread half of the bread cubes evenly in the prepared baking dish. Brush with 1½ tablespoons of the melted butter. Pour the pear mixture, including the pan juices, over the top, spreading evenly. Scatter the dried cranberries over the pears. Spread the remaining bread cubes over the top, and brush with the remaining 1½ tablespoons butter.

❀ In a large bowl, whisk the eggs well until blended. Whisk in ½ cup (3 oz/100 g) of the brown sugar, the almond extract, the nutmeg, and the salt. Add the half-and-half and mix thoroughly to incorporate the sugar into the liquid. Ladle the egg mixture evenly over the bread and pears.

❀ Cover the top of the pudding with a sheet of waxed paper and place 2 heavy plates or another baking dish on top to weight down the contents. Let stand for 10 minutes. Remove the weight(s) and waxed paper and cover the dish with plastic wrap. Refrigerate for at least 4 hours or for up to overnight.

❀ When ready to bake the pudding, preheat an oven to 350°F (180°C). Remove the plastic wrap and sprinkle the top with the remaining ¼ cup (2 oz/60 g) brown sugar. Bake until the top is golden brown and a knife inserted into the center comes out clean, about 1 hour. Remove from the oven and let cool for 5–10 minutes. The pudding will have puffed up during baking, but will settle as it cools.

❀ Cut the warm pudding into 10 portions, transfer to individual plates, and serve.

NUTRITIONAL ANALYSIS PER SERVING: Calories 607 (Kilojoules 2,549); Protein 14 g; Carbohydrates 83 g; Total Fat 25 g; Saturated Fat 13 g; Cholesterol 185 mg; Sodium 606 mg; Dietary Fiber 4 g

Chocolate-Orange Brownies

PREP TIME: 35 MINUTES

COOKING TIME: 35 MINUTES,
    PLUS 30 MINUTES FOR
    COOLING

INGREDIENTS

FOR THE BROWNIES

¼ cup (2 fl oz/60 ml) orange juice

⅔ cup (4 oz/125 g) raisins

5 oz (155 g) semisweet (plain)
    chocolate, cut into small pieces

½ cup (4 oz/125 g) unsalted butter,
    cut into small chunks

2 eggs

¾ cup (6 oz/185 g) sugar

¾ cup (4 oz/125 g) all-purpose
    (plain) flour

1½ teaspoons grated orange zest

½ teaspoon baking powder

½ cup (2 oz/60 g) chopped walnuts

FOR THE GLAZE AND GARNISH

2 oz (60 g) semisweet (plain)
    chocolate, cut into small chunks

2 tablespoons unsalted butter

2 teaspoons orange-flavored liqueur
    such as Grand Marnier

16 orange zest strips, each ¼ inch
    (6 mm) wide

MAKE-AHEAD TIP: Because these
brownies are so moist, they keep well.
Store in an airtight container at cool
room temperature for up to 3 days.

Serve these scrumptious cakelike brownies after a soup-and-
sandwich meal or pack them for a picnic supper in the park.

MAKES 16 BROWNIES

✤ Preheat an oven to 350°F (180°C). Butter an 8-inch (20-cm) square
baking pan and then dust with flour. Tap out the excess flour.

✤ To make the brownies, pour the orange juice into a small saucepan
and place over medium heat just to warm. Place the raisins in a small
bowl, pour the warm juice over them, and let stand until plumped,
8–10 minutes.

✤ In a heatproof bowl, combine the chocolate and butter. Set over
(but not touching) simmering water in a saucepan and melt, stirring,
until smooth. Remove from over the water and set aside.

✤ In a bowl, using an electric mixer set on medium speed, beat the eggs
until blended. Gradually add the sugar in a thin stream and continue
to beat until the mixture is pale yellow and thickened, about 2 minutes.
Reduce the speed to low and beat in the melted chocolate mixture. Then
add the flour, orange zest, and baking powder and beat in until incorporated. Stir in the plumped raisins and any remaining orange juice and
the walnuts. Pour into the prepared pan. Using a rubber spatula,
smooth the surface.

✤ Bake until firm and a wooden pick inserted into the center comes out
lightly coated but not wet, about 30 minutes. Transfer the pan to a rack
to cool to room temperature, about 30 minutes.

✤ While the brownies are cooling, make the glaze: In a small, heavy
saucepan over low heat, combine the chocolate and butter. Melt, stirring, until smooth. Stir in the orange liqueur. Remove from the heat
and let cool slightly to spreading consistency.

✤ Spread the glaze evenly in a thin layer over the top of the cooled
brownies. Let rest until set, then cut into 16 portions. Garnish each
brownie with a twisted strip of orange zest.

NUTRITIONAL ANALYSIS PER BROWNIE: Calories 250 (Kilojoules 1,050); Protein 3 g;
Carbohydrates 31 g; Total Fat 14 g; Saturated Fat 7 g; Cholesterol 47 mg; Sodium 27 mg;
Dietary Fiber 1 g

Apple-Raisin Cobbler with Maple Cream

PREP TIME: 30 MINUTES

COOKING TIME: 40 MINUTES

INGREDIENTS

3½ lb (1.75 kg) firm, tart apples such as Granny Smith, peeled, halved, cored, and cut into wedges ½ inch (12 mm) thick (about 8 cups)

1¼ cups (10 oz/315 g) granulated sugar, plus 1–1½ teaspoons for dusting pastry hearts

¼ cup (1½ oz/45 g) all-purpose (plain) flour

2 tablespoons unsalted butter, cut into pieces

½ teaspoon ground cinnamon

⅓ cup (2 oz/60 g) raisins

¼ cup (2 fl oz/60 ml) brandy

1½ teaspoons grated lemon zest

1 sheet frozen puff pastry, about 9 inches (23 cm) square and ⅛ inch (3 mm) thick (half of a 17¼-oz/535-g package frozen puff pastry), thawed in the refrigerator

FOR THE MAPLE CREAM AND GARNISH

1 cup (8 fl oz/250 ml) heavy (double) cream

2 tablespoons pure maple syrup

confectioners' (icing) sugar

COOKING TIP: Dark rum or calvados can be used in place of the brandy. Maple-walnut ice cream can be substituted for the maple cream.

The cobbler filling is first cooked on the stove top and then transferred to a baking dish. Separately baked puffed pastry hearts are used in place of the typical biscuit topping.

SERVES 6

❀ Position an oven rack in the lower third of an oven and a second rack in the center of the oven. Preheat to 400°F (200°C). Lightly butter a 1½–2-qt (1.5–2-l) baking dish.

❀ In a large, heavy, deep saucepan over medium heat, combine the apples, 1¼ cups (10 oz/315 g) granulated sugar, flour, butter, and cinnamon. Cook, stirring constantly, until the fruit gives off juice and starts to soften and the mixture thickens, about 10 minutes. Remove from the heat and stir in the raisins, brandy, and lemon zest. Mix well and pour into the prepared dish. Place on the center rack in the oven and bake for 15 minutes.

❀ Meanwhile, place the puff pastry sheet on a floured work surface. Using a rolling pin, roll over it just enough to smooth out any folds. Using a heart-shaped (or other decorative) cookie cutter 2½ inches (6 cm) in diameter, cut out 12 hearts. Place on an ungreased baking sheet. Brush the pastry hearts with a little water and sprinkle lightly with granulated sugar.

❀ When the cobbler has baked for 15 minutes, place the baking sheet holding the pastries on the lower rack in the oven. Bake until the pastries are puffed and lightly golden and the cobbler is hot and bubbly, about 10 minutes. Remove the cobbler and pastries from the oven and, using a spatula, transfer the pastries to the top of the cobbler. Return the cobbler to the center rack and bake until the pastries are a rich golden brown, 3–5 minutes longer. Watch carefully, as the pastries can burn easily. Remove from the oven and let rest for 10 minutes.

❀ Meanwhile, make the maple cream: In a chilled bowl, whip the cream until soft peaks form. Gradually whip in the maple syrup, beating until firm peaks form.

❀ To serve, dust the cobbler with confectioners' sugar and cut into 6 servings. Transfer to dessert plates and top with maple cream.

NUTRITIONAL ANALYSIS PER SERVING: Calories 817 (Kilojoules 3,431); Protein 5 g; Carbohydrates 120 g; Total Fat 35 g; Saturated Fat 14 g; Cholesterol 66 mg; Sodium 120 mg; Dietary Fiber 6 g

Strawberry-Almond Tart

PREP TIME: 30 MINUTES,
PLUS 30 MINUTES FOR
CHILLING CRUST

COOKING TIME: 25 MINUTES,
PLUS 15 MINUTES FOR
COOLING CRUST

INGREDIENTS

FOR THE CRUST

½ cup (2½ oz/75 g) blanched almonds, coarsely chopped

3 tablespoons sugar

1 cup (4 oz/125 g) plus 2 tablespoons cake (soft-wheat) flour

6 tablespoons (3 oz/90 g) chilled unsalted butter, cut into chunks

1 egg yolk

1 tablespoon cold water

½ teaspoon almond extract (essence)

FOR THE FILLING

¼ lb (125 g) cream cheese, at room temperature

½ cup (4 oz/125 g) lemon curd

2 pt (1 lb/500 g) small or medium strawberries, hulled

⅓ cup (3½ oz/105 g) red currant jelly

PREP TIP: Small or medium berries work best in this recipe because they can be left whole for placing attractively on the filling. If only larger berries are available, you will need to slice them before arranging them on top.

Plump, juicy strawberries top this lovely tart, which looks far more complicated to assemble than it actually is. The almond-seasoned dough is made in a food processor, patted into a tart pan, and quickly baked. The filling is store-bought lemon curd whisked into cream cheese.

SERVES 8

❂ To make the crust, in a food processor, combine the almonds and sugar. Pulse until the nuts are finely ground, about 1 minute. Add the flour and pulse briefly to mix. Scatter the butter pieces over the flour mixture and pulse until the mixture resembles coarse meal. In a small bowl, whisk together the egg yolk, water, and almond extract. Pour the mixture through the feed tube as you continue using on-off pulses, then pulse only until the dough forms a rough ball.

❂ Remove the dough from the processor and gather it together. Flour your hands to prevent sticking, then press the dough evenly into the bottom and up the sides of a 9-inch (23-cm) tart pan with a removable bottom. Cover with plastic wrap and refrigerate until firm, about 30 minutes.

❂ Preheat an oven to 375°F (190°C).

❂ Prick the bottom of the crust with a fork. Bake for 10 minutes. Prick the crust again and bake until it is golden brown and has begun to shrink from the sides of the pan, about 15 minutes longer. Transfer to a rack to cool completely, about 15 minutes.

❂ While the crust is baking, make the filling: In a bowl, using an electric mixer or a whisk, beat the cream cheese until smooth. Gradually beat or whisk in the lemon curd until completely incorporated and the mixture is smooth. Spread the cheese mixture evenly in the bottom of the cooled crust. Decoratively arrange the berries, stem ends down, on top.

❂ In a small, heavy saucepan over low heat, warm the jelly until liquefied. Brush the melted jelly carefully over the berries to glaze them. Serve immediately, or let stand at cool room temperature for up to 1 hour before serving.

NUTRITIONAL ANALYSIS PER SERVING: Calories 346 (Kilojoules 1,453); Protein 6 g; Carbohydrates 40 g; Total Fat 20 g; Saturated Fat 9 g; Cholesterol 65 mg; Sodium 61 mg; Dietary Fiber 2 g

Coconut Pound Cake with Vanilla Ice Cream and Warm Chocolate Sauce

PREP TIME: 35 MINUTES

COOKING TIME: 1½ HOURS

INGREDIENTS

FOR THE CAKE

1½ cups (7½ oz/235 g) all-purpose (plain) flour

½ teaspoon baking powder

⅛ teaspoon salt

¾ cup (6 oz/185 g) unsalted butter, at room temperature

1¼ cups (10 oz/315 g) sugar

3 eggs

½ cup (4 fl oz/125 ml) milk

1 teaspoon vanilla extract (essence)

½ cup (2 oz/60 g) sweetened coconut flakes

FOR THE TOPPING AND GARNISH

¼ cup (1 oz/30 g) sweetened coconut flakes

¾ cup (6 fl oz/180 ml) heavy (double) cream

6 oz (185 g) semisweet (plain) chocolate

1½ teaspoons vanilla extract (essence)

1 qt (1 l) good-quality vanilla ice cream

MAKE-AHEAD TIP: This cake keeps well for 2–3 days. Wrap tightly in plastic wrap and store at cool room temperature.

Here, traditional pound cake ingredients—butter, sugar, flour, eggs—are enhanced by the addition of sweetened coconut flakes. Bake the cake for a reunion of old friends.

SERVES 8

❀ Preheat an oven to 325°F (165°C). Butter a 9-by-5-by-3-inch (23-by-13-by-7.5-cm) loaf pan and then dust with flour. Tap out the excess flour.

❀ To make the cake, in a bowl, sift together the flour, baking powder, and salt. Set aside.

❀ In another bowl, using an electric mixer set on medium speed, beat the butter until creamy. Continuing to beat, gradually add the sugar in a thin stream, then beat until the sugar is incorporated and the mixture is pale yellow and smooth, about 8 minutes. Add the eggs, one at a time, beating well after each addition. Reduce the speed to low and beat in the flour mixture in three batches alternately with the milk, beginning and ending with the flour mixture. Stir in the vanilla and coconut. Pour the batter into the prepared pan. Smooth the surface with a rubber spatula.

❀ Bake for 1 hour. Reduce the oven temperature to 300°F (150°C) and continue to bake until a tester inserted in the center comes out clean, about 20 minutes. Remove from the oven and let stand in the pan for 10 minutes. Raise the oven temperature to 350°F (180°C). Using a knife, loosen the edges of the cake from the pan sides and unmold onto a rack. Turn right side up and let cool completely.

❀ To make the topping, spread the coconut on a baking sheet and place in the oven. Toast, stirring occasionally, until light golden brown, 4–5 minutes. Remove from the oven and pour onto a plate.

❀ In a heavy saucepan over low heat, stir together the cream and chocolate until the mixture is smooth. Stir in the vanilla and keep warm.

❀ To serve, cut the cake into 8 slices, each ¾ inch (2 cm) thick. Place each slice on a dessert plate and top with vanilla ice cream. Drizzle with the chocolate sauce, sprinkle with coconut flakes, and serve.

NUTRITIONAL ANALYSIS PER SERVING: Calories 839 (Kilojoules 3,524); Protein 10 g; Carbohydrates 93 g; Total Fat 50 g; Saturated Fat 31 g; Cholesterol 205 mg; Sodium 181 mg; Dietary Fiber 3 g

Extra-Thin, Extra-Crisp Oatmeal Cookies

PREP TIME: 20 MINUTES,
PLUS 15 MINUTES FOR
BATTER TO REST

COOKING TIME: 1 HOUR

INGREDIENTS

1 cup (3 oz/90 g) old-fashioned or
quick-cooking rolled oats

1 cup (8 oz/250 g) sugar

2 tablespoons plus 2 teaspoons
all-purpose (plain) flour

½ teaspoon salt

½ teaspoon baking powder

1 egg

1 teaspoon vanilla extract (essence)

½ cup (4 oz/125 g) unsalted butter,
melted and cooled

PREP TIP: It is important to let the
cookie batter rest for 15–20 minutes.
This allows time for the liquids—
butter and egg—to have a chance
to be absorbed by the flour and oats,
which results in a thicker batter.

Slim and crisp rather than thick and chewy, these oatmeal
cookies can be made up to 3 days ahead of serving. For a real
treat, serve them with Caramel Coffee with Cinnamon Cream
(page 15), or set them out where guests hit with a late-night
snack attack can find them.

MAKES ABOUT 4½ DOZEN 3-INCH (7.5-CM) COOKIES

✸ In a bowl, stir together the oats, sugar, flour, salt, and baking powder.
In another bowl, beat the egg and vanilla with a fork until just blended.
Add the egg mixture to the oat mixture and mix thoroughly. Add the
butter and stir just until combined. The batter will be very moist. Let
rest, stirring occasionally, for 15–20 minutes.

✸ Meanwhile, preheat an oven to 325°F (165°C). Line 2 large baking
sheets with parchment (baking) paper.

✸ Drop the batter by teaspoonfuls onto the prepared baking sheets,
spacing the cookies at least 2½ inches (6 cm) apart. Bake, one sheet
at a time, until the cookies have spread and are golden, 8–12 minutes.
Watch carefully, as they burn easily.

✸ Remove from the oven and slide the parchment with the cookies onto
a work surface. Let cool until firm, about 5 minutes. Peel the cookies
off the parchment and set them on a rack to cool completely. Continue
to bake the cookies in this manner, cooling the baking sheets between
batches, until all the batter is used. (The parchment can be reused.)
Store in an airtight container at room temperature for up to 3 days.

NUTRITIONAL ANALYSIS PER COOKIE: Calories 40 (Kilojoules 168); Protein 0 g;
Carbohydrates 6 g; Total Fat 2 g; Saturated Fat 1 g; Cholesterol 9 mg; Sodium 27 mg;
Dietary Fiber 0 g

Old-Fashioned Peach Icebox Pie in a Gingersnap Crust

PREP TIME: 25 MINUTES

COOKING TIME: 40 MINUTES,
PLUS 1½ HOURS FOR
COOLING AND CHILLING

INGREDIENTS

FOR THE CRUST

1¼ cups (5 oz/155 g) gingersnap
cookie crumbs

¼ cup (2 oz/60 g) unsalted butter,
at room temperature

3 tablespoons sugar

FOR THE FILLING

2¼ lb (1.1 kg) firm but ripe peaches
(about 6)

1 cup (8 oz/250 g) sugar

3 tablespoons cornstarch (cornflour)

3 tablespoons lemon juice

FOR THE GARNISH

1 cup (8 fl oz/250 ml) chilled heavy
(double) cream

1 peach

1–2 gingersnap cookies, crushed to
make crumbs

Make this rich pie at the height of peach season. The easy ginger-snap crust is filled with cooked peaches seasoned only with sugar and lemon, and the topping is swirls of plain whipped cream. Do not count on any leftovers!

SERVES 6–8

❋ Preheat an oven to 375°F (190°C). Butter a 9-inch (23-cm) pie dish.

❋ To make the crust, in a food processor, combine the crumbs, butter, and sugar. Pulse until the butter is evenly distributed and the mixture starts to clump together. Remove from the processor and press the mixture onto the bottom and sides of the prepared pie dish.

❋ Bake until the crumbs begin to brown, about 8 minutes. Transfer to a rack and let cool. When cool enough to touch, press down gently on the crust to push the crust up along the sides of the dish.

❋ To prepare the filling, peel and pit the peaches. Cut into slices ¼ inch (6 mm) thick and place in a colander to drain for 10 minutes. Put half of the peach slices in a heavy saucepan and crush well with a pastry blender or potato masher. Stir in the sugar, cornstarch, and lemon juice. Place the pan over medium heat and cook, stirring constantly, until the mixture starts to bubble. Reduce the heat to low and cook, stirring, until the mixture thickens and turns clear, 5–8 minutes. Remove from the heat and let stand until cool, about 30 minutes.

❋ When the mixture is cool, stir in the remaining peach slices. Pour the filling into the crust, cover, and refrigerate for at least 2 hours or for up to overnight.

❋ To make the garnish, in a chilled bowl, using an electric mixer or whisk, whip the cream until firm peaks form. Using a rubber spatula, spread the whipped cream over the pie filling, forming attractive swirls. Cover and refrigerate for 1–3 hours before serving.

❋ When ready to serve, peel, halve, and pit the peach and cut lengthwise into slices ½ inch (12 mm) thick. Arrange the slices in a decorative border over the cream. Sprinkle the cookie crumbs over the pie and serve.

NUTRITIONAL ANALYSIS PER SERVING: Calories 487 (Kilojoules 2,045); Protein 3 g; Carbohydrates 73 g; Total Fat 22 g; Saturated Fat 13 g; Cholesterol 66 mg; Sodium 158 mg; Dietary Fiber 3 g

GLOSSARY

ASPARAGUS

Tender shoots of asparagus start pushing up through the earth in early spring and reach their peak of flavor in May. Choose spears with tightly closed buds and with stem ends that look freshly cut.

AVOCADOS

The best-tasting and among the most widely cultivated avocado variety is the **Hass**, which comes into season in spring and summer. Easily distinguished by its pearlike shape and very pebbly, greenish black skin, it has buttery-smooth green flesh when perfectly ripe.

CHEESES

Their ability to add rich flavor and texture to many dishes makes cheeses a versatile staple for weekend entertaining. Those used in this book include:

BLUE CHEESE

A wide variety of blue-veined cheeses are enjoyed on their own or as ingredients. Among the most renowned is Roquefort, a French sheep's milk cheese noted for its creamy consistency and sharp taste.

FONTINA

This popular Italian cheese has a firm, creamy texture and delicate, nutty taste.

GOAT CHEESE

Sharply tangy goat cheeses, also known by the generic French term *chèvre*, are made

BERRIES

Plump and sweet, fresh berries are one of the delights of the weekend table. Spherical, smooth-skinned **blueberries** (at right) flourish from early June through mid-summer; juicy red, purple-black, or golden **raspberries** are harvested throughout summer, but are at their best at midseason; and **strawberries**, distinguished by their deep pink to red heart shapes, thrive from early spring to early summer.

CHOCOLATE

For many people, chocolate is the quintessential treat, which makes it ideal for featuring in desserts and baked goods to welcome weekend guests. Seek out the best-quality chocolate available. Many serious cooks prefer brands from Belgium, Switzerland, or France, such as Callebaut, Tobler, or Valrhona. **Semisweet chocolate**, also known as plain chocolate, may be eaten on its own or used

in innumerable varieties. The types most commonly available are fresh and creamy and sold formed into small rounds or logs.

GRUYÈRE

A specific type of Swiss cheese, Gruyère has a relatively strong flavor, firm, smooth texture, small holes, and a reddish brown rind.

MONTEREY JACK

A soft, mild, buttery cow's milk cheese first developed in Monterey, California.

PARMESAN

The firm, well-aged cow's milk cheese of Italy is classically used for grating. The finest

in recipes; it is usually, but not always, slightly sweeter than products referred to as **bittersweet chocolate**, which may be used in its place. Ivory-hued **white chocolate**, although it resembles chocolate in texture and richness, does not contain any chocolate solids. Used for both eating and cooking, it is made by combining pure cocoa butter, the source of its color and richness, with sugar, powdered milk, and occasionally vanilla.

COCOA POWDER

An almost fat-free source of rich chocolate flavor in sweets and beverages, this unsweetened powder is ground from the solids left after much of the cocoa butter has been extracted from roasted and ground cocoa beans. Cocoa specially treated to reduce its natural acidity, resulting in a darker color and more mellow flavor, is known as Dutch cocoa or **Dutch-process cocoa**.

CORN

With its sweet and mellow flavor, fresh corn is one of the greatest culinary pleasures of summer and early autumn. For the best quality,

variety, designated Parmigiano-Reggiano®, is made only from midspring to mid-autumn, then aged for more than a year.

PEPPER JACK

This form of jack cheese (see left) is distinguished by the addition of crushed hot chile.

PROVOLONE

This Italian cow's milk cheese has a fairly firm texture, a pale yellow color, and a slightly sweet and smoky flavor.

RICOTTA

This light-textured, white, very mild cheese, used in savory and sweet recipes, is produced from whey left over from making other cheeses. Sheep's milk is the traditional base, although cow's milk ricotta is more common.

buy recently harvested corn at farmers' markets and roadside stands, which are likely to offer the freshest selection. Pull back the green husks and fine silks, which themselves should look fresh and pale, to check that the kernels are plump and smooth.

CORNMEAL, YELLOW

Ground from dried kernels of yellow corn, this granular flour, sometimes known by the Italian term *polenta,* has a sweet, robust flavor. Stone-ground cornmeal, made from whole corn kernels, has the richest taste and most distinctive texture.

COUSCOUS, INSTANT

This staple of the North African table is made from semolina formed into tiny beads. It cooks to a fluffy consistency for serving as an accompaniment to stews or other saucy dishes. From-scratch couscous can take more than an hour to steam, but well-stocked food stores sell an "instant" product that has been precooked and redried and cooks in only a few minutes.

CURED PORK

Preserved and flavored by salting, brining, or smoking, many different kinds of cured pork products find their way onto the weekend table, most often as part of breakfast or brunch menus. For the most robust **bacon,** cured from the rich and tender pork belly, seek out thickly cut slices from a butcher shop or counter rather than the prepackaged variety.
Pancetta (at right), a specialty of Emilia-Romagna in northern Italy, is an unsmoked bacon cured with salt and pepper.  The Italian cured ham known as **prosciutto,** a specialty of Parma, has an intense flavor and deep pink hue. It is best appreciated in tissue-thin slices as an appetizer or chopped to flavor sauces and stuffings. Among the most legendary of smoked hams is the German **Black Forest** variety, admired for its rich, smoky-sweet flavor and firm, tender texture.

HERBS

Intensely aromatic and packed with flavor, herbs introduce a vivid, graceful note to whatever they season. When grown in a kitchen garden or window box, they can be easily harvested to enhance a special weekend meal.

BASIL

Spicy-sweet, tender-leaved basil, an essential seasoning in Mediterranean cooking, complements poultry, tomatoes, and other vegetables.

CHIVES

When you are seeking an onionlike flavor without the bite, reach for chives. Mild and sweet, they are at their best when fresh and raw, as cooking diminishes their flavor.

CILANTRO

Also known as fresh coriander and Chinese parsley, cilantro has flat, frilly leaves that resemble those of flat-leaf (Italian) parsley. Its flavor is astringent, slightly grassy, and a little bitter.

MINT

Refreshingly sweet, mint is a popular seasoning for lamb, poultry, vegetables, and fruit. Spearmint is the type most widely sold.

OREGANO

Also known as wild marjoram, this highly aromatic herb, a staple of Italian and Greek cooking, is used dried or fresh in all kinds of savory dishes. It marries especially well with tomatoes.

PARSLEY, FLAT-LEAF

Also known as Italian parsley, this variety of the widely popular fresh herb, native to southern Europe, has a more pronounced flavor than the common curly type, making it preferable as a seasoning.

ROSEMARY

Used either fresh or dried, this Mediterranean herb has a strong, aromatic flavor well suited to meats, poultry, seafood, and vegetables.

SAGE

Whether used dried or fresh, soft, gray-green sage leaves are pungent and aromatic. They go particularly well with poultry, vegetables, and pork.

THYME

One of the most important culinary herbs of Europe, thyme delivers a light fragrance and flavor to a variety of foods. Its subtly minty flavor complements vegetables and nearly every meat and fish.

FENNEL BULBS

Looking remarkably like a small head of celery squashed down into a fat bulb, fennel is paler green than celery but has the same stringy outer layer. Its texture is clean and crisp, and its flavor is reminiscent of mild, sweet anise. Look for bulbs with the feathery leaves intact and bright green, a sign of freshness.

HARICOTS VERTS

This French term refers to young summer green beans that are harvested when very tender and very thin.

LEEKS

Succulent and with a delicate, sweet onion flavor, leeks arrive in the market in late summer and extend their stay through spring. The blanched white base, more tender and more delicately flavored than the green leaves, is most often used alone, served as a cooked vegetable in its own right or added to other savory dishes. The tougher greens can be used to flavor stocks or other long-cooking dishes. To remove grit trapped in the multi-layered leaves, make a lengthwise slit from the root end to the point where the white part meets the green tops, then rinse thoroughly in cold water.

MAPLE SYRUP, PURE

The breakfast and brunch syrup of choice as well as a potent sweet flavoring, maple syrup is the boiled sap of the sugar maple tree, enjoyed for its rich, sweet taste and caramel brown color. Look for products labeled "pure" maple syrup, avoiding those that are diluted with cane or corn syrup. Pure maple syrups are graded by color, with the finest, designated Fancy Grade, a light amber with correspondingly delicate taste.

MOLASSES

A source of rich, earthy sweetness in baked goods, molasses is a thick, syrupy by-product of refining cane sugar.

MUSHROOMS

With their earthy flavor and satisfying chewy texture, mushrooms of all sorts lend a robust, luxurious quality to a wide variety of savory dishes. Look for both cultivated and wild mushrooms at well-stocked food stores, greengrocers, and farmers' markets.

Portobello mushrooms (above), the fully matured form of brown-skinned, ivory-fleshed cremini mushrooms, are distinguished by their large, flat, circular brown caps, which grow to 4 inches (10 cm) or larger in diameter. When cooked, they have a rich, almost meaty taste and texture. Parasol-like **shiitake mushrooms** (below) were once found

only in Asia, but are now cultivated all over the world. The thick, flat caps have a firm, meaty texture. Discard the tough stems before using. **White mushrooms**, the most common cultivated mushroom variety, are available abundantly and inexpensively year-round. They are enjoyed for their ivory color and clean, mild flavor.

MUSTARD, DIJON

Traditionally made in the French city of Dijon from dark brown mustard seeds (unless otherwise marked *blanc*) and white wine or wine vinegar, Dijon mustard has a distinctive pale color and moderately hot, sharp flavor.

OILS

A variety of good-quality oils plays a fundamental role in the kitchens of creative cooks. **Olive oils** range in flavor from spicy with a peppery kick to buttery and mellow. Those labeled "extra virgin" are generally fruity and full flavored and are suitable for dressing salads and for use as a condiment. Oils labeled "pure" are blended and good for cooking. **Asian sesame oil**, pressed from roasted sesame seeds, is used primarily as a seasoning or condiment. Do not confuse it with the lighter, cold-pressed sesame oil sold in health-food stores and well-stocked food stores. In recipes, the term **vegetable oil** applies to seed and vegetable oils, such as **canola**, **safflower**, and **corn**, that are relatively flavorless and may be heated to the high temperatures necessary for frying.

OLIVES, KALAMATA

A specialty of Greece, these pungent, brine-cured black olives are packed in vinegar. They may be found in ethnic markets and well-stocked food stores.

ONIONS

All kinds of onions lend pungent flavor to savory dishes. **Green onions**, also called spring onions or scallions, are a variety harvested immature, leaves and all, before their bulbs have formed. **Red (Spanish) onions** are a mild, sweet variety with purplish red skin and red-tinged flesh.

POTATOES

These popular tubers are distinguished by size, shape, the color and thickness of their skins, and the color and texture of their flesh. Early in the year, look for **new potatoes**, small, immature specimens that are harvested when their skins are fragile and their waxy flesh is delicate and sweet. **Red potatoes** are generally small and have white, waxy flesh and red skins. **Yukon gold potatoes** have fine-textured flesh known for its golden color and rich, buttery flavor.

SHALLOTS

These coppery-skinned cousins of the onion have a more delicate flavor than their pungent kin. The finely textured flesh is most commonly used as an aromatic seasoning.

SPICES

Aromatic seeds, berries, buds, roots, and barks are all used as spices. Grinding them releases their essential oils, so buy whole spices whenever possible and grind them as needed in an electric spice mill or in a mortar with a pestle. Buy already ground spices in small quantities and store airtight at cool room temperature.

CAYENNE PEPPER

Prized for its hot taste and bright red color, this fine powder is ground from the dried cayenne chile.

CHILI POWDER

A commercial blend of spices containing ground dried chiles along with such other complementary ground seasonings as cumin, oregano, cloves, and coriander. Do not confuse it with "pure chile powder," which is finely ground dried chile alone.

CINNAMON

One of the most popular spices for baked goods and other desserts, cinnamon is the aromatic bark of a type of evergreen tree. It may be bought either ground or as whole dried and curled strips of bark, known as cinnamon sticks.

TOMATOES

Look for vine-ripened tomatoes in food stores and farmers' markets at their summertime peak. For especially sweet, juicy flesh, select bite-sized, yellow or red round **cherry** or **teardrop-shaped tomatoes.** For year-round use, use the Italian **plum** variety, also known as the Roma tomato, which is roughly the size and shape of an egg. It has reliably good flavor and texture, whether fresh or canned.

CLOVES

Native to Southeast Asia, these dried flower buds of an evergreen tree have a rich, highly aromatic flavor and may be used whole or ground.

CUMIN

These potent, crescent-shaped seeds and the fine, greenish brown powder ground from them have a strong, dusky aroma and flavor.

CURRY POWDER

A blend of spices most often used to season Indian dishes. The typical ingredients are coriander, cumin, chile, fenugreek, and turmeric.

GINGER

Although ginger resembles a root, this seasoning is actually the underground stem, or rhizome, of the tropical ginger plant. In both its fresh and its ground dried forms, ginger has a sweet-hot flavor that enhances savory and sweet dishes alike.

NUTMEG

The hard pit or seed of the fruits of the nutmeg tree, this popular sweet spice adds a subtle dimension of flavor to both sweet and savory dishes. Nutmeg may be bought already ground, but the freshest, fullest flavor comes from grating the whole nutmeg as needed.

WATERCRESS

A member of the mustard family, these crisp sprigs of round, dark green leaves contribute a refreshingly spicy flavor to salads and make a distinctive garnish for other dishes.

RED PEPPER FLAKES

The coarsely crushed flesh and whole seeds of dried red chiles, these flakes contribute a touch of moderately hot flavor to sauces and other preparations.

SAFFRON THREADS

It takes the hairlike stigmas from many thousands of blossoms of a specific variety of crocus to yield 1 pound (500 g) of this golden, richly perfumed spice, one of the world's most expensive. Fortunately, just a pinch of saffron will impart a bright, sunny color and heady aroma to a dish. Look for saffron threads, the whole dried stigmas; avoid ground saffron, which loses its flavor more rapidly.

TURMERIC

This popular Asian spice, widely available already ground, is a rhizome (underground stem) with a mildly pungent, earthy flavor. It lends a bright yellow color resembling that of saffron to whatever it seasons.

INDEX

almonds
   and dried cherry streusel coffee cake 22
   -strawberry tart 101
apple-raisin cobbler with maple cream 98
apricot walnut muffins, double- 36
asparagus, fettuccine with Brie and 64
avocado, shrimp, and tomato salad with lime vinaigrette 41

bacon, peppered, country omelets with 20
bananas
   sautéed, cinnamon French toast with 33
   -strawberry smoothies 14
beans
   grilled tuna, white bean, and arugula salad 50
   sliced flank steak, haricot vert, and potato salad 60
   Texas-style chili 78
   white, butternut squash soup with 59
beef
   grilled flank steak with horseradish mashed
      potatoes 73
   sliced flank steak, haricot vert, and potato salad 60
   Texas-style chili 78
beverages 14–15
blueberry sauce, lemon pancakes with 25
bread pudding, warm pear and dried cranberry 94
brownies, chocolate-orange 97
burgers, turkey, with jack cheese 55
butternut squash soup with caramelized onions 59

cake, coconut pound, with vanilla ice cream 102
caramel coffee with cinnamon cream 15
carrot, mushroom, and leek soup 45
cheese
   Brie, fettuccine with asparagus and 64
   cream, scrambled eggs with smoked salmon and 26
   fontina and prosciutto sandwiches, grilled 42
   goat, minted, tomato soup with 38
   Parmesan, gratin of eggs with mushrooms, rosemary,
      and 34
   pepper jack cornmeal pancakes with tomato salsa 30
   pizza with tomatoes, olives, and pancetta 86
   ricotta, lasagne with spinach, prosciutto, and 81
cherry, dried, and almond streusel coffee cake 22
chicken
   garlic-rubbed baguette with tomatoes, tapenade, and 46
   lemon-scented roasted 63
   pappardelle with caramelized onions, rosemary, and 85
chili, Texas-style 78
chocolate
   -orange brownies 97
   pudding with toffee pecan crumble 92
   sauce, warm, coconut pound cake with 102
   white and dark hot 15
cobbler, apple-raisin, with maple cream 98
coconut pound cake with vanilla ice cream 102
coffee, caramel, with cinnamon cream 15
coffee cake, dried cherry and almond streusel 22
cookies
   chocolate-orange brownies 97
   extra-thin, extra-crisp oatmeal 104
corn and lobster chowder 53
couscous with a vegetable mélange 66
cranberries, dried
   -and-orange scones 29
   and pear bread pudding, warm 94

eggs
   country omelets with potatoes, leeks, and peppered
      bacon 20
   gratin of, with mushrooms, rosemary, and Parmesan 34
   scrambled, with smoked salmon and herbed cream
      cheese 26

fennel, pasta salad with oranges, watercress, and 49
fettuccine with Brie and asparagus 64
fish. See also salmon
   grilled tuna, white bean, and arugula salad 50
   seafood stew with tomatoes, shrimp, and scallops 74
   skewers of swordfish, red peppers, and oranges 82
French toast, cinnamon, with sautéed bananas 33

honey and jalapeño grilled salmon 70

lamb chops, pepper-and-cumin-coated 77
lasagne with spinach, prosciutto, and herbed ricotta 81
leeks
   country omelets with potatoes, peppered bacon, and 20
   mushroom, carrot, and leek soup 45
lemon
   -mint tea coolers 14
   pancakes with blueberry sauce 25
   -scented roasted chicken 63
lobster chowder, corn and 53

menus, planning 16–17
muffins, double-apricot walnut 36
mushrooms
   gratin of eggs with rosemary, Parmesan, and 34
   mushroom, carrot, and leek soup 45

oatmeal cookies, extra-thin, extra-crisp 104
omelets, country, with potatoes, leeks, and peppered
   bacon 20
oranges
   chocolate-orange brownies 97
   -and-cranberry scones 29
   -ginger pork tenderloins 69
   pasta salad with fennel, watercress, and 49
   skewers of swordfish, red peppers, and 82

pancakes
   lemon, with blueberry sauce 25
   pepper jack cornmeal, with tomato salsa 30
pancetta, pizza with tomatoes, olives, and 86
pappardelle with chicken, caramelized onions, and
   rosemary 85
pasta
   couscous with a vegetable mélange 66
   fettuccine with Brie and asparagus 64
   lasagne with spinach, prosciutto, and herbed ricotta 81
   pappardelle with chicken, caramelized onions, and
      rosemary 85
   salad with oranges, fennel, and watercress 49
peach icebox pie, old-fashioned 107
pear and dried cranberry bread pudding, warm 94
pepper jack cornmeal pancakes with tomato salsa 30
peppers, red, skewers of swordfish, oranges, and 82
pie, old-fashioned peach icebox 107
pita pockets with pork, red onion, and chutney mayonnaise 56
pizza with tomatoes, olives, and pancetta 86
plum gratin, warm 91
pork
   pita pockets with red onion, chutney mayonnaise, and 56
   tenderloins, orange-ginger 69

potatoes
   country omelets with leeks, peppered bacon, and 20
   horseradish mashed, grilled flank steak with 73
   sliced flank steak, haricot vert, and potato salad 60
prosciutto
   and fontina sandwiches, grilled 42
   lasagne with spinach, herbed ricotta, and 81
puddings
   chocolate, with toffee pecan crumble 92
   warm pear and dried cranberry bread 94

raspberries
   sauce, ginger waffles with 19
   and strawberries, warm compote of 89

salads
   grilled tuna, white bean, and arugula 50
   pasta, with oranges, fennel, and watercress 49
   shrimp, avocado, and tomato, with lime vinaigrette 41
   sliced flank steak, haricot vert, and potato 60
salmon
   honey and jalapeño grilled 70
   smoked, scrambled eggs with herbed cream cheese
      and 26
sandwiches
   garlic-rubbed baguette with chicken, tomatoes, and
      tapenade 46
   grilled fontina and prosciutto 42
   pita pockets with pork, red onion, and chutney
      mayonnaise 56
   turkey burgers with jack cheese 55
scallops, seafood stew with tomatoes, shrimp, and 74
scones, cranberry-and-orange 29
seafood stew with tomatoes, shrimp, and scallops 74
shrimp
   seafood stew with tomatoes, scallops, and 74
   shrimp, avocado, and tomato salad 41
smoothies, banana-strawberry 14
soups
   butternut squash, with caramelized onions 59
   corn and lobster chowder 53
   mushroom, carrot, and leek 45
   tomato, with minted goat cheese 38
spinach, lasagne with prosciutto, herbed ricotta, and 81
squash soup, butternut, with caramelized onions 59
strawberries
   -almond tart 101
   -banana smoothies 14
   and raspberries, warm compote of 89
swordfish, red peppers, and oranges, skewers of 82

tart, strawberry-almond 101
tea coolers, lemon-mint 14
tomatoes
   garlic-rubbed baguette with chicken, tapenade,
      and 46
   pizza with olives, pancetta, and 86
   salsa, pepper jack cornmeal pancakes with 30
   seafood stew with shrimp, scallops, and 74
   shrimp, avocado, and tomato salad 41
   soup with minted goat cheese 38
   Texas-style chili 78
tuna, white bean, and arugula salad, grilled 50
turkey burgers with jack cheese 55

waffles, ginger, with raspberry sauce 19
walnut muffins, double-apricot 36
white and dark hot chocolate 15

ACKNOWLEDGMENTS

The publishers would like to thank the following people and associations for their generous support and assistance in producing this book:
Desne Border, Ken DellaPenta, Kathryn Meehan, Anna Preslar, Vivian Ross, and Hill Nutrition Associates.

The following kindly lent props for photography: Ma Maison, San Francisco. The photographer would like to thank Rebecca Stephany for generously sharing
her home for location photography. She would also like to thank ProCamera, San Francisco, CA; and FUJI film for their generous support of this project.